Chambers

SCOTTISH
DRINK BOOK

A cargo of liquid gold leaves the Laphroaig island distillery.

(John Hume)

Chambers

SCOTTISH

DRINK BOOK

whisky, beer, wine and soft drinks

Contributors:
Jan Fairley, Jack Gillon,
Charles McMaster and Michael Moss

Acknowledgements

Scottish drink is distinctive for its wide range and high quality. The study of Scottish drink through to the present day has been a fascinating one, shedding light on more than simply a nation's drinking habits. The authors are deeply grateful to the many people within the Scottish drinks industry whose knowledge of their subject and generous contribution of their time have made this book possible.

The authors would also like to thank the following people for their help and support: John Hume, co-author with Michael Moss of *The Making of Scotch Whisky*; the late Ross Wilson, whose extensive papers on whisky are now deposited in Glasgow University archives; Charles Craig, Chairman of Invergordon Distillers; John A. R. Macphail, Chairman of Robertson & Baxter; Ian Reed of United Distillers; Dr Ian Donnachie; Ann Halliday; J. D. Lawrie; and the Scottish Brewing Archive, Heriot-Watt University.

Additionally the authors would like to thank Thérèse Duriez for editing the manuscript, Tracey Francis for correcting the proofs and Alastair Fyfe Holmes of Chambers for helping to make the project a reality.

© Carter Rae Editorial Services 1990

Published 1990 by W. & R. Chambers Ltd, 43–45 Annandale Street, Edinburgh

British Library Cataloguing in Publication Data
Chambers Scottish drink book.
 1. Scotland. Drinks
 I. Moss, Michael S. (Michael Stanley), *1947-*
 641.2'09411

ISBN 0-550-20003-7

Produced by Carter Rae Editorial Services
Design and layout by F M Artwork and Design
Cover design by James Hutcheson
Typeset by Hewer Text Composition Services, Edinburgh
Colour origination by Bordercolour, Brampton, Cumbria
Printed in Great Britain by The Eagle Press PLC

Contents

Introduction

When you think of Scotland you inevitably think of the country's most famous product – whisky. The very mention of 'Scotch' conjures up an image of landscape, of mist-covered hills and glens and clear, bubbling water filtering through peat and along the beds of stony streams.

Scotland is, however, equally distinguished for its beer and soft drinks. Brewing began with the ancient Picts, noted makers of spruce and heather beers, and was later developed by the religious orders in Border abbeys such as Melrose and Dryburgh. Soft drinks as we know them today took longer to arrive. It was the Victorians, with their penchant for sweets, who popularised ginger beer, the forerunner of a whole range of fruit-flavoured drinks.

Wine, too, has an historical role in the country's diet despite the fact that the Scottish climate is hostile to the cultivation of vineyards. It may have been Victorian grocers who started the tradition of making spiced wines in their back rooms but centuries before that, as a consequence of the Auld Alliance between Scotland and France, the wines of Bordeaux were consumed in such quantity that they could well have laid claim to being the national drink. Claret carts rattled through the streets of Edinburgh dispensing wine to all comers and not even tax could halt the flow. It could be said that the city once 'ran' on the juice of the grape – in 1692 one-third of its corporate income was derived from the duty on wine.

The Port of Leith, where the wine was landed, was also the site for other famous events connected with Scottish beverages. It was here in 1835 that the clipper *Isabella* landed with the first shipment of China tea from the Far East. It was also to Leith that the first shipment of Caribbean limes arrived – the basis of a famous cordial originally created to prevent sailors from catching scurvy.

Scotland's greatest asset in terms of its commercial drinks industry is its water. Much romanticism and mystique surrounds this natural resource but few deny its importance. Whether bottled at source or used in the manufacture of whisky or beer, Scottish water is hard to match for purity and taste. King James IV acknowledged this fact in 1488 when he paid the then large sum of twelve shillings for ale made from a local spring in Perthshire.

The production of whisky and beer has remained largely unchanged over the years although new technology has speeded up the process of malting, fermentation and distillation. The ingredients for both drinks remain identical – fresh Scottish water, malted barley and yeast. What has changed is public demand. The availability of drinks has often been governed by wars, taxes and trade barriers. But 'fashion' and social pressures also make an impact. French wine may once have been a cheap drink for the masses, but chocolate as a drink was popularised by the upper classes, who thought it 'exotic'. The number of breweries in Scotland in 1840 – some 280 – also give us a clue to the universal appeal of that particular drink. The pubs of the time, however, were not so appealing – especially to 'respectable' ladies. For them, the arrival of the tea garden was a more desirable alternative. Developed as the acceptable focus of family outings, tea gardens and rooms became the place where everyone, maid servant and mistress alike, could sit over tea, bread and butter and cakes and be entertained with music.

Whisky, of course, has also fluctuated in popularity. Originally a drink that was only produced and consumed in the Highlands, Scotch whisky has become one of the country's most popular ambassadors. Eighty-five per cent of all whisky distilled in Scotland today is sent abroad, accounting for, by the end of 1989, close to £1.5 billion annually in revenue. Until the recent emphasis on healthy eating and drinking, the Americans took the largest portion – 25 per cent – of these exports. Conversely, with sales to the United States declining, sales to the French have increased dramatically – France is now the second largest importer of whisky. Perhaps another tribute to the Auld Alliance?

The number of whiskies available – especially the blends – seems infinite. Unlike the brewing industry which has contracted, the consumer is spoiled for choice when it comes to whisky. And at home, despite the increased demand for mineral waters (which the Scots can happily accommodate) and fruit juices, not to mention the appearance of alcohol-free wines and beers, the allegiance to whisky has proved stable over the last decade. Some 45 million litres of pure alcohol are distilled annually for the home whisky market alone.

A country's culture is not simply its art, literature, theatre and music, but its food and drink as well. These tell us about the quality of life, both past and present, and about the ways in which people have survived. In Scotland, the centuries have seen radical changes in drinking patterns and tastes. Ale and wine were once the drink of the poor, while chocolate and coffee could only be bought by the rich: today the wide range of Scottish-made drinks is available to everyone. This book, written by a team of experts, draws a comprehensive picture of the past and present of Scotland's favoured drinks, explaining their history and their making in an unprecedented way. Its conclusion is clear: Scotland's culture is not only alive and well, but distinctive, strong and unique.

> If all be true that I do think
> There are five reasons we should drink;
> Good wine – a friend – or being dry –
> Or lest we should be by and by –
> Or any other reason why.
> *Dean Aldrich, 1647–1710*

1. Water – The Essential Link

> Water is good; it benefits all things and does not compete with them.[1]

Scottish water has an unbeatable reputation and its importance to the drinks industry cannot be overstressed. The breweries of Glasgow and Edinburgh flourished with the pure, soft water of the Lowlands while, in the Highlands, water that had trickled through peat became an essential ingredient of Scotch whisky. The country's mineral water is also renowned. The Victorians discovered the benefit of mineral water first in the spas – a health-conscious public today enjoys it in bottles.

The abundance of this natural resource was not always appreciated. For centuries the ordinary folk of Scotland preferred to drink ale or cheap wines from France because water supplies were so badly affected by the inadequate disposal of sewage. In the Shetland Isles, north of mainland Scotland, those who could not afford ale might drink Bland. Made from the whey of milk, Bland could not be distinguished from 'best mountain wine' if, once prepared, it was left 'in the skiow hut until winter – [then] take it down and drink

Opposite: A talented skateboarder jumps over his Irn-Bru.

(Della Matheson)

Below: Highland water comes from springs in the hills. The Ochil Hills in Perthshire are kept completely free from farming, fertilisers and pesticides.

(Highland Spring)

9

in families – it is fine and stout – mix in a little sugar'. According to 'a gentleman' writing an *Account of White Herring Fishing* in 1758, the recipe was as follows:

> Take freshly churned milk and remove the butter. Heat two to three large rounded stones and put on top of the churn. The thicker part of the liquid will fall to the bottom. Pour out the thin liquid into vessels. This is Bland. Eat the thick part like curds. Drink the thin part or pour into casks and carry to a hut on a hill called a 'skiow' and leave to mature.[2]

Traicle Ale was also popular, especially when milk supplies fell low in the countryside and in winter. Brewed in a big crock or wooden tub it contained treacle, barm (yeast) and water. When sufficiently fermented it was put into bottles and used instead of milk with morning porridge to give flavour – with 'quite a kick if the traicle ale was well fermented!'[3] More recently this century there was Inkie Pinkie, a kind of ginger beer immortalised in the rhyme 'Hinkey-pinkie, Jaw sticker toffee . . . lemon-kali boxes, all four a penny'.[4] And Boston Cream which was often made up at the corner shop out of boiling water, sugar, egg white, tartaric acid, bicarbonate of soda and lemon essence.[5]

Chocolate

With the exploration of the New World, the Far East and Africa in the fifteenth, sixteenth and seventeenth centuries came not only silver and gold but also a lucrative trade in tea, coffee and chocolate. At first, the drinking of such delicacies was restricted to the court and the upper classes but by the seventeenth century world mercantile trade had developed further and a home market had begun to open up.

The first 'exotic' drink to become popular in Scotland was chocolate.[6] In London, Samuel Pepys mentioned the drink in his diary in 1664: 'to a Coffee-house, to drink jocolatte, very good,' and by June 1674 there was a 'Chocollatte house' in Edinburgh – but it was an expensive drink at three dishes for six shillings (30p). Chocolate found great favour with the upper classes and particularly, it seems, with the ladies. There are many recorded descriptions of special drinking pots with their own stirrers. In 1681 there was in Hamilton Palace 'a jaculatt pot and stik', the stick presumably for stirring the drink into a froth.[7]

Chocolate came by sea from the ports of Holland and London. Direct trade in cocoa beans began after 1655 when Britain captured Jamaica where the Spaniards had considerable plantations of cacao trees. It was bought by gentry like the Duchess of Hamilton who purchased 'six pounds (2.5 kg) of the finest cake jocolet' in 1689.[8]

By the mid-eighteenth century its use was on the wane as it was superseded by tea and to a lesser extent coffee. Chocolate regained popularity in the nineteenth century when the process of defatting cocoa made powdered drinking chocolate available, leading to a more widespread use by all classes.

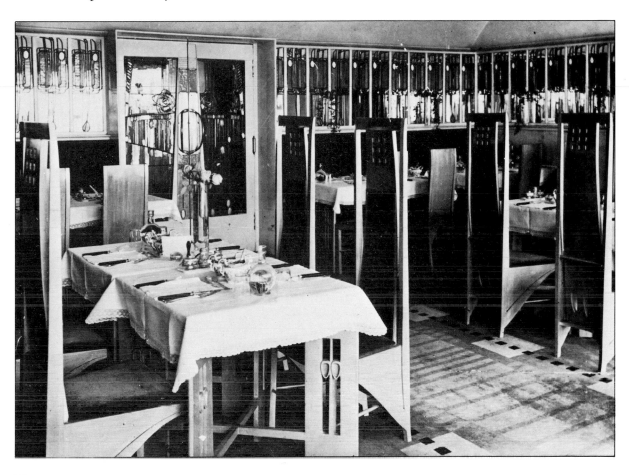

Tea

Tea drinking became popular in the seventeenth century when there were not only repressive laws against the imported wine of the upper classes but also in 1725 an extension of the malt tax of Scotland. Successive governments, however, were quick to profit by the imposition of Excise duty on tea.[9] The tax was enormous, much higher than the present VAT.

For a long period the East India Company held an import monopoly and controlled the auctions from the elegant surroundings of East India House in London. But high prices led to weak brews and smuggling on a national scale involving the respectable as well as the dishonest. A 'blind eye' was turned to the whole thing by nearly everyone. Even the clergy were involved – indeed the crypt of the Parish Church was a favourite, safe hiding place. Tea was

The 'Room de Luxe' at Miss Cranston's Willow Tea Rooms was designed in the Scottish Art Nouveau style by Charles Rennie Mackintosh.
(Hunterian Art Gallery, University of Glasgow, Mackintosh collection)

taken off merchant ships by local fishermen who hid their boats in caves connected to remote lanes, snickets and bridleways which can still be found in the Fife ports of Pittenweem, Anstruther and St Monans today. Eventually the scale of the smuggling undermined the East India Company and their monopoly was ended.

The primary justification for the drinking of tea was its supposed medicinal values. Tea was first sold from apothecary shops, reflected in the names of many of today's popular brands: Typhoo is the Chinese word for doctor; PG Tips stood for Pre-Gestive tips and 99 Tea was known as doctor's or prescription tea. In 1673 the Earl of Lothian wrote from London to his Countess telling her he had been ill of an ague but was better after 'drinking tea and warme water and forsing myself to vomite'. In his diary, Hay of Cam'nethan reports that tea was introduced into Edinburgh when James, Duke of York, brother of Charles II, visited Holyrood Palace and the Duchess introduced the 'heart-opening cordial' to her guests. By 1675 small amounts were being brought into Scotland: Provost Robert Mylne of Linlithgow imported four pounds (1.8 kg) at a cost of 88 guilders in May 1675 for the Duchess of Linlithgow but the cost of tea remained so steep that even at the highest social levels only small quantities were bought.[10] The actual making of tea was a technique still being learned in the early years of the eighteenth century.

Drinking tea several times a day is now so commonplace, with the advertisement 'everything stops for tea' more a truth than a fiction and factory tea breaks institutionalised, that it is hard to believe that two hundred years ago tea drinking among the lower classes was denounced from many a pulpit! It was alleged that, like smuggled spirits, it would corrupt the poor. One Law Lord maligned tea as a 'vile drug'. And those who liked their morning draught of ale regarded it as effeminate, as suggested by Mackintosh of Borlum's complaint of 1729:

When I came to my friend's house in the morning, I used to be asked if I had my morning draught yet? I am now asked if I have had my tea? And in lieu of the big quaigh (bowl) with strong ale and toast, and after a dram of good, wholesome Scots spirits, there is now the tea-kettle put to the fire, the tea table and silver and china equipage brought in, and marmalade and cream.[11]

Although tea replaced good ale, milk and plain water, even at the end of the eighteenth and into the nineteenth century ministers of the Church continued to denounce tea drinking amongst farm labourers (and their wives): it was ranked with wheaten bread as an unnecessary luxury, a waste of wages. Actually, improvements in farming meant cottagers ceased to keep milk cows as in earlier days. At the same

Opposite: At Melroses in Leith, taster Nigel Conquest performs an hourly tea tasting.

(Della Matheson)

time high duties on malt and beer made these too expensive for such folk. Such factors inevitably meant that they were 'driven to substitute tea . . . an enervating liquor . . . the only thing like luxury, which their circumstances could afford'.[12] However in 1750 Dr Thomas Short had published a 'Discourse on Tea' recommending it for its 'eminent and unequalled Power to take off, or prevent Drowsiness and Dullness, Dammps and Clouds on the Brain and intellectual Faculties'. And by 1810 it had made its way everywhere: 'a tea equipage on a small scale has also of late become an indispensable article of cottage furniture'. Country shops began to package it in $\frac{1}{2}$ penny portions with $\frac{1}{4}$ pennyworth of sugar to go with it. And amongst farmworkers the traditional breakfast of porridge and milk (or some oatmeal dish) was replaced by the far less nourishing one of tea with bread and butter.

Public tea drinking began in Coffee Houses, fashionable places for the upper classes and wealthy merchants to meet. By 1750, when it was more commonplace, even though a pound of tea (450g) would have cost a skilled worker perhaps a third of his weekly wage, tea was also being drunk in Tea Gardens. Sunday was the big day when tradesmen, maidservants, apprentices and well-to-do arrived on family outings and paid an entry fee to drink tea, eat bread and butter, watch illuminations and fireworks, promenade and listen to music.

By the turn of the century Glasgow was better endowed with quality tearooms than London, many remarkable for their interior decoration. The most famous were Miss Cranston's Willow Tea Rooms in Sauchiehall Street designed in Scottish Art Nouveau style by Charles Rennie Mackintosh. Mackintosh provided a total environment from the characteristic high backed chairs to specially designed china, tea spoons, cutlery and tables, which were covered with 'fair white cloths set with flowers'. The scones and cakes which filled the three-tier cake stands to be eaten with specially blended tea were legendary! In Edinburgh in the same period ladies took their tea in Jenners cream and gold Tea Rooms where they too could drink a special blend called 'Old Edinburgh'. Both cities boasted a large number of other popular tearooms and coffee houses.

It must be a remnant of the early East India Company monopoly that while tea comes from all parts of the world to be blended and packaged in both Scotland and England it is considered to be quintessentially 'English' as opposed to British! Tea has always been an important Scottish drink with significant Scottish importers and blenders.

At the family firm of Drysdales in Edinburgh the tea buying, tasting, blending and selling process has continued in essence relatively unchanged since 1878. Each weekday at Drysdales in a small room in a back street of Edinburgh, an old-fashioned kettle is filled with cold fresh mains water and placed on a gas burner. On one side of a

Opposite: Melroses' original hand-written ledgers from 1815 remain on display at the company offices.

(Melroses Limited)

Edinburgh 1815.

90

Dr Bramwell & Aitkenson's Card Contra Cr

1815											
Nov	14	To Cash	103	14	–	3	June	16	By Goods p D Book	44	14 0 3
1816 May		To Cash		27	18	7	Sept	18	By Ditto	58	13 – 2
Nov	27	To Do		10	1	6	Oct	18	By Ditto	120	14 18 –
"		To Do		17	2	7	August	8	By Ditto	242	10 1 6
							October	9	By Ditto	277	47 2 7
1817				£55	2	3	1817				£55 2 3
June	4	To Cash	424	31	15	4	Feby	7	By Goods	349	31 15 4
Dec	3	To Do	21	5	18	–	July	3	By Blue	445	5 18 –
July	13	To Do	31	20	1	4	March	16	By Do	142	20 – 4
Janre	9	To Do	85	7	11	10	Sept	15	By Do	392	7 11 11
July	20	To Do	469	13	1	"	March	10	By Do	216	13 1 –
Aug	16	To Casks returnd	523	13	6		Aug	4	By Blue	522	26 0 1
1820	17	To Broke Blue	525	14							
Jany	31	To Cash	95	24	12	7					
				£104	6	7	(a/o to folio 89)				£104 6 7

Dr Rickett & Marshall Hull Contra Cr

1815							1815				
Oct	4	To Cash	86	5	3	–	June	9	By Goods p D Book	41	5 3 –
April	5	To do		14	8	–	Nov	6	By Do	99	14 8 –

Dr Lord Meadowbank Royal Circus Cr

1823		From folio		8	6½	1823 July	31	By Cash	437	10 18 0½
June	10	To Goods	333	3 17 6						
			£10 18 0½	£10 18 6½						£10 18 0½

Dr Robt Megget Pennycuick Contra Cr

1815							1815				
Sept	7	To Goods p D Book		"	7	7½	June	21	By Goods p Day Book	215	" 14 1
1816 July	19	To Cash	230	4	–	3½	"	28	By Ditto	220	" 17 4
							July	5	By Ditto	223	" 7 4
							"	11	By Ditto	226	" 17 4
							"	19	By Ditto	230	1 2 9
			£4 8 10								£4 8 10
June	11	To Goods	372	"	6	4	June	19	By Cash	365	10 6
	18	To Goods	383	"	4	2					
			£ – 10 6								£ – 10 6

15

small traditional set of brass hand scales an old weight is set while on the other exact amounts of different types of tea leaves are weighed in turn and then deposited in old highly glazed pottery cups with lids. As the kettle reaches boiling point it is removed from the heat and the water poured onto a selection of teas brought from China, Sri Lanka, Sumatra, Java and Assam in India – from tea gardens with names like Laxapana, Thumaita and Kinora. After four to five minutes the tea is poured into matching chunky white cups and the tasting begins. A sample from each cup is supped from individually warmed spoons.

One of the first things you notice as you bring the different spoons in turn to your lips and smell the delicious aroma is the different colour of each tea. The next thing you notice is the different taste. By drawing in a lot of air with the tea and making a fabulous slurping noise, the tea tickles the taste buds in every part of your mouth so that you are tasting it with the maximum stimulation of your palate. Breathing out sharply through the nose the tea is then spat directly into a spittoon and you move on to the next tea sample, listening to the connoisseurs uttering words like 'astringent', 'malty', 'penetrating yet delicate', 'smoky', even 'ah, champagne'. When you turn out the empty brewing pots and press the leaves it is surprising how the textures of each tea vary – particularly tea from China where growing and picking processes have remained orthodox and unchanged for centuries.

Tea plantations are usually situated at high altitudes where the soil is volcanic. Once the camellia bush is ready to be harvested, the leaves are picked, dry roasted and shipped within 24 hours. Each tea chest that is imported into Scotland represents part of a single day's picking from one field. Fields are harvested in rotation and every day's crop is different on the same estate. Tea is re-tasted when it arrives at the factory and its characteristics recorded by the blender so that he knows what is available when it comes to making up blends.

The constant factors that tea tasters consider are taste, colour and body – also price, availability and the amount that can be supplied in order to maintain as consistent a standard in the tea supply as possible. As many as 60 teas can be used to maintain a blend although the average is closer to 15. The role of the blender is to keep the blend as stable as possible to keep the customer happy.

As well as orthodox tea (dried leaves with a shredded rolled shape, graded into different sizes), there is tea which is rolled and cut to produce pellet-like shapes called 'Cut Tear and Curl' (CTC). This comes mainly from Africa. With no leaf the tea infuses quickly in the pot: finer grades are used for tea bags. Most Scottish tea suppliers will tell you that the quality of tea supplied for bags is always good. It is the temperature of the water and method of making tea (those dreadful coin operated tea machines) which ruin the flavour: even low grade and 'dust' teas are vigilantly controlled by the Tea Council.

Melroses, another Edinburgh firm, have been situated in an old whisky bond warehouse in Couper Street, on the Water of Leith, since 1921. It was in 1812 that Andrew Melrose established himself as a wholesale grocer, tea dealer and merchant in the Canongate in the centre of the city. As the shop was open from 7 am until 10 pm six days a week the staff lived in! His early newspaper advertisement in the *Edinburgh Evening Courant* of Saturday 24 April 1819 mentions 'black tea at 4s 8d (23p) a 1 lb (450g), green tea at 6s 4d (32p) a 1 lb, and gunpowder tea at 10s 6d (52p)' with the added news that Melroses' brokers included Mr Larken, Chief Inspector of tea to the East India Company in Canton China: 'none can surpass him in experience and knowledge of that article'. By 1820 Melroses had a wholesale warehouse in Drummond Street and premises in Princes Street and George Street. Because of high rates and other considerations these were sold in the 1960s. Today Melroses package 1500 tons (1524 tonnes) of tea a year and 500 million tea bags!

Andrew Melrose was the first Scottish merchant to organise legal tea shipments to arrive in Britain outside the port of London. Melrose chartered the 422-ton (427 tonnes) fore-top sail schooner *Isabella*,

Melroses have been hand-packing tea for as long as anyone can remember.
(Della Matheson)

Tea-packers at work in the past. The Leith factory has been modernised, but the structure of the former whisky warehouse still remains.

(Melroses Limited)

owned by the Edinburgh wine and spirit merchants Hutchison and Company. She sailed to Canton, China under Master Captain Robertson on 2 December 1833, returning to Scotland in April 1835 with 7000 chests of tea only to set sail again for China in May of the same year.

Andrew Melrose's son, William, went out and based himself in China dealing directly with brokers and transport. By 1837 Melroses were granted a Royal Warrant by Queen Victoria to supply tea and coffee to royal households in Scotland. This warrant has been renewed by each monarch. Melroses continue to package many pure teas, and prepare blends like the delicious 'Old Edinburgh' for Jenners. They also still supply many quality grocers with loose tea.

Tea has to be kept in dry, odourless conditions because it absorbs strong smells. Today Melroses has all the latest equipment ingeniously organised to make maximum use of many floor levels within its historic listed Leith building. Although taken over by Premier Brands in 1986 the factory continues to function much as it did when still a family company.

Tea bags dominate 80 per cent of the market, with Edinburgh firms supplying extensive ranges on contract to other companies in the United Kingdom and institutions throughout Scotland. Most of the tea bags are 'tagged, bagged or packaged' with different brand names. Both Melroses and Drysdales continue to supply a wide range of pure teas like Darjeeling and Lapsang Souchong (which gains its distinctive taste being smoked over charcoal) and Tippi Golden Orange Flavoury Pekoe. Earl Grey is a perennial British favourite (its distinctive perfumed flavour comes from spraying oil of Bergamot onto keenum leaf). Lemon tea is created by simply blending lemon with the leaves. Jasmine tea is a blending of 'green' China teas, which are manufactured without allowing the leaf to fully oxidise before firing: dried jasmine flowers are added to give its distinctive slightly bitter perfumed taste. Newer herbal teas (not to be confused with pure herbal infusions) have names like 'Wild and Mild' which has cinnamon added and 'Hedgerow' with apple.

Coffee

Coffee was probably discovered over 1000 years ago in Ethiopia when a goatherd noticed that his goats had become unusually active after nibbling the red berries off the nearby bushes! It did not reach Scotland in any great amount until the eighteenth century although in 1687 James Mclurg of Edinburgh sent an order to Holland: 'Sir, my nices has a coffee house which ther servants keepes and stands in neid of some Coffie berrie . . . try the lowest pryce and buy anc barrell full of it that will hold 100 (45kg) or 150 lb (68kg)'.[13]

Over time, coffee has been thought to have a therapeutic effect on diseases such as dropsy, gout, scurvy, stomach trouble, coughs, consumption, kidney stones, malaria and even typhoid fever. It came to Europe by the caravanserai through Syria, Turkey and Greece. Few people realise that in terms of international trade today coffee ranks as second to oil as the most valuable commodity.

Coffee, like tea, grows on volcanic soil in sheltered and rainy areas in tropical countries like Costa Rica, Nicaragua, Bali and Kenya. It is the sun dried, green beans, the fine flavoured Arabica and coarser, harder flavoured Robusta which are brought to Scotland to be blended and roasted. At Drysdales it is tasted in the same room as the tea and under similar conditions. The weight used is different: on the scales for coffee is placed an old penny circa 1920! Two-hundred-pound measures of coffee, pure or blended, are roasted at a time. The beans are sucked up into a circular hopper and dropped into a rotating roaster. Litres of cold water are then injected to cool the beans. The smell is wonderful! Roasted to order, the coffee leaves the factory within hours – it is never allowed to sit on the shelf.

Highland Spring's attractive bottles, with their distinctive tartan and thistle label, grace the best tables.
(Highland Spring)

Water

Water is the main element of all Scottish drinks. Spring water has long been used to help the functioning of the liver and kidneys and purify the system. Until 1833 mineral waters were considered medicines. Only then were they exempted from levies and they could be consumed both as a refreshment and for medicinal purposes. Until the twentieth century town and river water was often unsafe. The small, unspoilt village of Blackford in Perthshire has been renowned for its water for centuries. King James IV stopped there in 1488 and paid the then great sum of 12 shillings (60p) for ale made from local water. Robert Barr, the head of the Barr family, remembers his father William spending time in Blackford learning how to brew ginger beer. Then there were at least five breweries situated in the village drawing on the water from the Ochil Hills.

Today Blackford is the home of the Highland Spring Water company. The efficient, beautifully designed factory with the latest equipment from Italy and France (where bottled water has of course been *de rigueur* for many years) draws water from six stainless-steel lined bores each drilled to about 330 feet (100 m) depth into the hills.

The water is pumped to surface level, gravity-fed to a central valve housing and piped down the hill to storage tanks at the back of the factory from where it is drawn directly into the bottling room. The ecologically-conscious owner bought the catchment area of 2000 acres (809 hectares), keeping it completely clear of farming so that no sewage, pesticides or nitrate fertiliser can seep into the water sources. Samples taken daily from each bore are subjected to various laboratory tests, including mineral content and radiation. Samples are also taken regularly from the 16–17 000 bottles which are filled each hour on a normal day. Little stock is held and the bottled water leaves the factory within hours of leaving the ground.

Mineral water is stringently controlled and constantly tested to ensure its stability. It cannot receive any treatment other than filtering and must be bottled at source. The only thing that can be added is carbon dioxide to make it lightly sparkling. Highland Spring now have their distinctive image including their own tartan.

Another significant Scottish mineral water producer is Strathmore, which nestles at the foot of the Grampian Mountains in the Vale of Strathmore in the Royal Burgh of Forfar. The Strathmore family home is Glamis Castle, the childhood home of Her Majesty The Queen Mother.

Glamis Castle in the Grampians, childhood home of Her Majesty the Queen Mother, is now the home of Strathmore Water.
(Strathmore Water)

Both Strathmore and Highland Spring bottle water for other customers who include many of the well-known supermarkets. At Highland Spring, each customer has his own dedicated borehole which draws water from a different position on the hill. No two waters are the same. Waters are largely defined by their mineral content which create their unique tastes, dependent on the geology of each area. Highland Spring percolates for approximately 30 years through basalt rock. The water from Strathmore's single 450 foot (136 m) borehole which seeps through red sandstone is roughly the same age.

Over the years many different shapes, sizes and types of bottles have been used for both water and soft drinks. Today, apart from the usual glass, plastic PET (Polyethylene Terephalate) and PVC are increasingly used.

Lime Juice

One of the most distinctive soft drink bottles that has stood the test of time is that belonging to Rose's Lime Juice, the world's first concentrated fruit drink. Although the juice is now a product owned by the vast Cadbury-Schweppes company (Swiss Jacob Schweppe was one of the first Europeans to carbonate water on a big scale, setting up in Bristol in 1794), the juice was first produced and bottled in Edinburgh.

Rose's Lime Juice is as delicious today as it must have been to the sailors who first drank it, sailing out of Leith. The 1867 Merchant Shipping Act compelled ship-owners and the Navy to provide crews with a daily dose of lime juice (rich in Vitamin C), to help prevent scurvy – the reason British sailors were nicknamed 'limeys'!

Rose's, initially a firm of Ships Chandlers in Leith, turned to importing the juice from the West Indies in the mid-1860s, acquiring estates in Dominica and planting limes on a large scale. Lachlan Rose was the member of the family responsible for patenting the process for preserving lime juice without the addition of the usual rum. Afterwards, the domestic market opened up. In this way L. Rose and Co. began 'furnishing delicious, cooling and refreshing beverages eminently wholesome for family use'. Rose's eventually owned and bought the harvest from the best lime tree plantations in the West Indies and Gold Coast (now Ghana).

The secret of Rose's unique flavour is a combination of the maturity of the fruit (seven years), the speed with which it is crushed as soon as it falls off the trees and the crushing process itself. The limes are selected and washed in clear running water and then crushed between giant granite rollers in a mill. Juice is either shipped in its raw state or clarified by filtering or racking.

Opposite: Barr's kept the memory of Iron Brew alive during wartime sugar shortages with a strip cartoon series featuring Ba-Bru and his friend Sandy. Iron Brew was relaunched after the War as Irn-Bru.

(A. G. Barr plc)

'Ginger'

Flavoured mineral waters began with the addition of herbs like dandelion and burdock. Artificially-carbonated or 'aerated waters' were first introduced in Scotland in the latter half of the eighteenth century and the origins of soda water can be traced to the same period. Local recipes for 'pop' or soft drinks which can be traced back several hundred years still abound. The *Dundee Courier* of 1987 gave an 'old recipe for *Sugarelly Water*':

> a stick of liquorice, or black-sugar, was chopped into small pieces, and these were dropped into a biggish bottle which was then filled with water. The bottle was shaken long and vigorously to get the liquorice to dissolve, and in time the water inside grew brown-black and frothy. To hasten the brew it was traditional to place the bottle in darkness of a cupboard or under a bed. A firm belief was held that the longer the stuff was left 'in bond', the richer and more mature it would become. Despite this it seldom lasted very long. Who could resist having a 'swig' every now and again?[14]

Stone ginger beer was a very popular drink in Scotland from the late eighteenth century until the Second World War. And it is ginger beer which bridges the gap between soda water and fruit flavoured drinks of commercial manufacture. It started as a 'home brew' and at the height of its popularity almost every small town had one or more small businesses selling their own brands. Over one thousand trade names for ginger beer have been recorded. Earlier this century Old Daw's ginger pop and milk stall used to be a feature on the Old Course in St Andrews. In fact the fourth hole on the Old Course is named Ginger Beer after Old Daw and his refreshment barrow. But while 'ginger' remains a much used name for fizzy drinks in many parts of Scotland it was a casualty not only of post-war fashion but of the War itself for only a few soft drinks factories remained open during the period and supplies of raw materials were limited.

Initially a firm's territory was limited by the distance a horse could walk out and back in a day, usually a radius of 16 kilometres (10 miles). In 1905 Falkirk had eleven 'mineral water' manufacturers as they were called, Ayr had five and Glasgow 37. Today Glasgow has only two! One of them is A. G. Barr, manufacturers of Scotland's most famous soft drink, Irn-Bru. First launched as Iron Brew in 1901, and then re-named Irn-Bru in 1946, the myth of its power comes from a 'secret recipe' involving fruit extract and iron salt. It remains a 'multi-million pound' secret locked in two men's minds and the bank vault. Only Robert Barr and his son Robin know what makes Scotland's 'other national drink'.

The reputation of Irn-Bru was built upon its restorative properties as a stimulating tonic. Long ago John Blair of Motherwell Football Club endorsed it saying 'the tonic properties in Barr's 'Iron Brew'

Opposite top: T-shirt from California, hat from Italy, Irn-Bru from Scotland.
(Della Matheson)

Opposite bottom: Barr's liquid sugar tanker follows a tradition of bold and witty advertising.

(A. G. Barr plc)

are just what every athlete requires, and I have much pleasure in recommending it to all who aspire to athletic fame'. Today in Scotland it is drunk by 44 per cent of those who buy soft drinks and it outsells Coca-Cola three to one. And Irn-Bru is not only drunk by children: it has an established reputation as a cure for a hangover!

When Robert Barr first began manufacturing and selling 'lemonade and aerated waters' in Falkirk in 1880 (when the family cork-making business was in decline), he little imagined that in the 1980s Barr's would employ 1800 people at 18 locations throughout the United Kingdom and that the company would be the biggest selling carbonated soft drinks manufacturers in Scotland with their products selling well abroad.

Barr may have originally gone into soft drinks because of the minimum investment capital needed but the company's reputation for zeal was established early on when family members studied brewing aspects of the soft drinks trade in remote country areas. The ingredients for soft drinks have changed little from the days when pure mains filtered water was mixed with cane sugar and citric acid and flavoured with orange, lemon, dandelion and burdock and sarsaparilla. Now, however, while cane sugar is still used there are also new products which use low calorie sugar substitutes for diabetics and slimmers.

Barr's have always been in the vanguard of soft drinks developments. Their publicity has been vigorous, witty, and appealing to the popular imagination. In 1901 they introduced a 'hairy Highland athlete' based on a gentleman from the north of Scotland. A 'less uncouth' athlete adorned Irn-Bru's special packaging from the 1930s until 1988 when a major new design was introduced. Barr's advertised the loss of Iron Brew during the War period as 'one of the hardships of the War effort'! After the War ended Iron Brew was re-launched as Irn-Bru and Barr's introduced strip cartoon characters called 'Ba-Bru and Sandy' whose exploits were avidly followed in newspaper columns. Sandy was a Scottish boy complete with tam-o-shanter and kilt while Ba-Bru was a black boy complete with turban and shorts. Eventually the well-loved pair gave way to television ads and the memorable dictum 'Irn-Bru — your other national drink'. Barr's sugar tanker, painted like an enormous Irn-Bru can, bears the legend 'Don't drink more than eighty gallons (363 litres) a day or you'll rust'.

Barr's have also remained leaders in bottling. They moved from the original corks they had made themselves to Hiram Codd's celebrated bottle with the marble stopper in the neck, perhaps the most ingenious closure ever applied to soft drinks. Barr's were the first to introduce the re-sealable screw-top, a real innovation which meant the fizz didn't disappear from the content of the bottles in half-an-hour. Today Barr's have moved far from the 1880s, when they filled clean empty whisky bottles. Now they use disposable bottles in response to supermarket demands. Although the custom for returning glass bottles is almost totally dead in England, it persists in Scotland, particularly in Glasgow and on the west coast. Regularly inspected and sterilised, glass bottles can be re-filled eight to nine times.

1989 saw the demise of the Barr's 'split', the favourite glass half bottle, particularly popular in fish and chip shops and holiday resorts. Although today Barr's can fill 5000 bottles an hour they continue to respond and cater for local regional tastes. Since taking over the Globe company of Edinburgh, based in a modern factory at Loanhead, they have continued to use the original Globe recipes for Globe label bottles because of the identified brand loyalty of a large number of their customers. Matching their respective local beginnings Globe remain more popular in the east of Scotland and Barr's in the centre and west. And while recently introducing new products like Pripps Energy Drink Barr's have also re-introduced old traditionals like dandelion and burdock, now available in cans!

The current President of Barr's who steered the company to public quotation and national status is distinguished 81-year-old Robert Barr (b. 3 September 1907). He can single-handedly chart the history of the soft drink industry in Scotland, remembering vividly places and faces as well as his own personal exploits.

With Lachlan Rose of Rose's, Robert Barr steered the committee which brought in high minimum standards and stringent rules for the soft drinks industry in Scotland after the War, helping to bring it safely into the modern world. He has watched his company move from the days of the limited territory of the horse drawn carts to today's ultra-modern business with a transport fleet covering the whole of the United Kingdom, with products reaching far flung parts of the world like Australia, where a shop in the outback sells all things Scottish including 'Oor Wullie' and Irn-Bru.

1.   *The Way of Lao Tzu*, trans. Wing Tsit Chan.
2.   *Account of White Herring Fishing*, London, 1758–9.
3.   *Dundee Courier*, 28 June 1980.
4.   *People's Friend*, 29 July 1950.
5.   *Dundee Courier*, 18 July 1983.
6.   Much of the information and the original historic research quoted for coffee, chocolate and tea comes (with kind permission) from an article by Dr Sandy Fenton, Research Director of the National Museum of Scotland entitled *Chocolate, Coffee and Tea in Scotland Seventeenth to Nineteenth Centuries*, originally presented at an Ethnological Food Conference held in Poland, autumn 1987 and to be published in the conference proceedings, forthcoming 1990.
7.   *Ibid.*, p.2.
8.   *Ibid.*, p.1.
9.   *Ibid.*, pp.6, 7.
10. *Ibid.*, p.8.
11. *Ibid.*, p.11.
12. *Ibid.*, p.12.
13. *Ibid.*, p.5.
14. *Dundee Courier*, 8 January 1987.

2. Wine and the Auld Alliance

In this country, wine seems necessary to inspire conversation after dinner.[1]

The legendary thirst of the Scots for claret almost came to an end in the latter part of Queen Victoria's reign. For hundreds of years the wines of Bordeaux had been drunk in such quantities, and by all and sundry, that they could almost have laid claim to being our national drink. George Saintsbury, then Professor of English at Edinburgh University and a renowned connoisseur, found that by 1880 a company of a dozen people could scarcely do justice to a magnum of claret, and when he left Edinburgh in 1915 he was forced to sell his cellar for a pittance.

Saintsbury, author of *Notes on a Cellarbook*, blamed smoking and the move towards a later dinner hour for the loss of interest in claret. There may well have been some truth in this, for claret had traditionally been used as an after-dinner drink, usually taken with olives, dinner being washed down with sweeter and heavier wines such as Madeira. The delicacy of claret would certainly take ill at being served in the atmosphere of a smoking room, but Gladstone's 1860 increase in tax on wine and the recent improvements in the quality of port were probably more significant factors.

In fact the decline was much more gradual than Saintsbury's observations might suggest and for at least a century before its demise claret could no longer have been considered a drink of the people. The first threat to the popularity of claret came with the Union of the Crowns and the Methuen Treaty which preceded it in 1703. As a symbol of English antagonism towards the French, the wines of France were taxed at a far higher rate than those of Spain and Portugal. This was still not enough to deter Scots from their beloved claret, and indeed throughout the eighteenth century they continued to drink it in prodigious amounts. Claret was Bonnie Prince Charlie's favourite drink (it was shipped direct to Inverness in those days) and the beverage helped to sustain Flora McDonald on her short but perilous voyage. Judges would have a bottle open in front of them on the bench, a practice which inspired no small amount of jealousy among the lower ranks of courtroom personnel, and drew a predictable, and probably justified, barrage of critical comment.

Firm and erect the Caledonian stood;
Old was his mutton, and his claret good;
'Let him drink port!' the English statesman cried –
He drank the poison, and his spirit died.[2]

A cargo arrives at Leith in the 1830s.
(Edinburgh City Libraries)

Penned defiantly by John Home at the end of the eighteenth century, this verse typified the Scots' attitude to the wines of Bordeaux in this period and was the clarion call of the very serious drinking that went on in Edinburgh in the clubs where political ferment and general outrageousness were the order of the day. In the seventeenth and eighteenth centuries it was the duty of a good host in Scotland to provide wine until the guests stopped drinking – and often this point was only determined by the onset of coma.

Whether it was part and parcel of enlightenment, or whether it was a direct result of the punitive rate of tax imposed in 1780, by the end of the eighteenth century claret (indeed French table wine, for burgundies were being mentioned in the chronicles of the latter half of the century, for the first time since the earliest days of Franco-Scottish commerce) was no longer the everyday drink of the people. It was apparently Scott's view that a new morality was at least partly to blame, and in 1825 he affirmed that drinking had ceased to be a common vice.

It scarcely seems credible that the delicate, dry wine of Bordeaux had been a staple drink in Scotland for centuries, a serious rival to whisky or beer, and that claret carts rattled through the streets of Edinburgh after a ship had disembarked at Leith. The wine was dispensed into whatever receptacle the customer provided, and was so cheap that little care was taken over quantities. Much that was written suggests that it was scarcely regarded as a seriously alcoholic drink, and indeed the quantities ordered for communion services even during the Reformation suggest that it took time for the old habits to die even among the religious zealots.

To understand this obsession we must go back to the roots of the Auld Alliance between Scotland and France. The English were in on the act at the beginning, annexing Gascony as a result of the marriage of Eleanor of Aquitaine to Henry Plantagenet in 1152. Bordeaux and its vineyards were English for three hundred years, but in the subsequent strife and eventual expulsion of the English, the Scots allied themselves with France. From the early part of the fifteenth century the King of France was protected by a personal troop of Scottish guards, *La Garde Ecossaise du Corps du Roi*, the name of which endured through the centuries, long after Scots had ceased to be part of it. The links between the countries were cemented by marriages, most notably that between Mary Queen of Scots and the Dauphin, and during her reign she reciprocated the French law granting automatic French citizenship to natives of Scotland living in France. These laws have never been repealed.

In 1138 the Vaults in Leith, which are still preserved, were mentioned in a charter granted by the Abbey of Holyrood during the reign of David I. The port of Leith continued to be the hub of the wine trade and claret was the bulk commodity. Scottish ships enjoyed fiscal privileges in Bordeaux, and also had the pick of the crop by virtue of being allowed to sail unhindered right into the Quai des Chartrons, while the English were forced to hand over their weapons at the mouth of the Gironde. Getting the wine to Scotland as fast as possible was vitally important in the days before corks made prolonged storage in bottles possible, and that wine which could not be consumed fresh was preserved by processes too horrible to describe. On 21 October 1659, a record was set for the earliest arrival of the new wine in Leith – a remarkable feat which must have engendered the same sort of interest and marketing success as our own Beaujolais Nouveau.

If the Scots enjoyed fiscal leniency in Bordeaux, the same was certainly not true at home. The first taxes on wine were imposed by James VI in 1612, yielding a revenue of £32 000. In 1692 one-third of Edinburgh's corporate income was derived from duty on the wine landed at Leith. From those far from dry statistics we can imagine the importance of wine in both social and commercial terms. It was not all about quantity, however, and by the early eighteenth century specific wines were being mentioned, for instance the Châteaux Haut Brion and Margaux offered by the Edinburgh merchants, Shairp and Houston, around 1715.

This tradition of connoisseurship endured through the excesses of that century and the rigours of the next, thanks to the lawyers on the one hand (they often ran their practices from taverns in the eighteenth century) and the literary intelligentsia on the other. Robert Louis Stevenson had a refined palate, his genuine interest in wine being revealed by a reference to the wines of the Napa Valley as 'these imperial elixirs' after his visit to California. Sir Walter Scott and the Cleikum Club were deservedly famous for their wine drinking, though it is surprising to learn that Scott himself was not particularly 'fine in the gab'. While he may have been no great connoisseur, Scott treated his friends generously to the best of champagne as well as prodigious amounts of claret. These were usually supplied by Cockburns of Leith, whose labels are still adorned by his image.

Drinking fine wine at its best is an art in itself.
(Della Matheson)

The Great Merchants of the Past

An elegant corner for the connoisseur at Cockburn's of Leith.

(Della Matheson)

George Cockburn was one of those sons of great families who were forced into commerce towards the end of the Georgian era. Cockburn was a natural businessman who did not restrict his interest to the light French wines that the Scots had always preferred. He spent some time in Portugal, and today the name is one of the many linking Scotland, perhaps somewhat ironically, with port, the archetypal English drink. Sandeman was the other entrepreneurial Scot who was highly influential in Oporto at the time, but the names Graham, Gould Campbell and Symington all testify to the Scottish influence.

Cockburn's of Leith continues to flourish to this day, now housed in an elegant and beautifully laid out shop in Edinburgh's North-West Circus Place. Their list is still dominated by claret and port, and it provides a very happy hunting ground for those seeking a wide range of quality allied to cunning selection born of so much cumulative wisdom, and a very fair pricing policy.

Few Scottish wine merchants can claim anything like the antiquity of Cockburn's, and Whighams of Ayr, founded in 1766, is the only one to predate them. James Oliphant, whose name the firm bore for many years, was astute 'enough to capitalise on the fact that Ayr was the Scottish port closest to the vineyards of southern Europe. He established a business associated largely with the great houses of the west of Scotland, and also forged trading links in Edinburgh. These exist to this day as Whigham's, whose present owners can claim direct descent from Oliphant, have a charming basement shop in North Castle Street. The association with the great houses still forms an important part of Whigham's business, and this, along with very high prices, has perhaps tended to foster a clubby, exclusive image which the firm is keen to disguise.

Wine Merchants Today

The purchasing of fine wine falls into clearly discernible patterns. Glasgow appears to constitute a huge black hole as far as fine wine drinking is concerned. If Glaswegians do drink fine wine, it is not clear where they buy it. Whighams have no outlet there, and one or two brave adventures in the mid-1980s came very rapidly to grief. Until recently the only ray of hope was the Ubiquitous Chip, a bohemian restaurant in the University area of Glasgow's West End. From the start it offered more interest and value on its wine list than on its menu and now there is also a Chip Wine Shop offering an interesting selection of wine at keen prices. And yet Glaswegians do not seem to beat a path to the shop in quite the numbers one might expect.

Puzzling, but not enough to deter Kathleen McMaster, a young enthusiast trained at the Chip, from going to manage d'Arcy's, a delightful little shop in the courtyard of Glasgow's most stylish shopping mall, Princes Square. The quality of wines on offer is beyond reproach yet business is slow and Kathleen, like everyone else who tries to sell fine wines in Glasgow, is still puzzled.

In 1674 there were no fewer than 34 independent wine merchants in Glasgow and heavy trade was reported from the fifteenth to the eighteenth centuries. There is surely a sleeping giant here, just waiting to be awakened by the right marketing approach.

Sixty-four kilometres away in Edinburgh, the giant never dozed off. True, merchants report difficulties in the fine wine trade in the past few years, in contrast with the boom years of the early 1980s, but there is still plenty of interest and no sign of the numerous independent merchants going to the wall despite the best efforts of the national chains. Oddbins, the most adventurous of these chains, owes its success to clever marketing and impressive buying power, but also to the accessibility of wines for browsers and the high standards of training given to young and enthusiastic staff.

The citizens of Edinburgh have never been slow to recognise a bargain when it comes to wine. Customers cram into Jimmy Hogg's tiny red, white and blue shop in Cumberland Street. The style suggests that nothing has changed since early Victorian times, but in fact the business is relatively young, having been started by Mr Hogg senior in the 1960s.

One of the older established independent merchants in Edinburgh is Peter Green and Co. in Warrender Park Road. Like Hogg, they have developed a national reputation for the quality and diversity of their list. The only other old-established shop to rival these two is G. Hush in Morningside Road, run by Mr McLeod and his son Rory – a happy hunting ground for those who like to get as much high quality wine as possible for their money.

Of the newer businesses, Raeburn Grocers in Comely Bank benefits from the enthusiasms of Zubair Mohammed, who has a passion for old wines and goes to great lengths to prise out rarities from growers whose confidence he has won. The philosophy and style of Wines from Paris, situated in the ancient cellars of the vaults of Leith, could scarcely be more different. Judith Paris runs her business as a mini-warehouse with a wholesale licence. Customers can browse at leisure among stacked cases, but they must buy by the dozen, albeit mixed.

One of the most 'up-and-coming' of the Edinburgh businesses is, curiously enough, one of the longer established. The legendary delicatessen of Valvona and Crolla at the top of Leith Walk has long had a faithful clientele among the locals as well as among Edinburgh's large Italian population, but it is only recently that anyone ever considered buying anything to drink from them apart from cases of the cheapest, most drinkable chianti. The change to a booming trade in the superb new-wave 'designer' Italian wines, such as those from Gaja in Piemonte or Zanelli in Lombardy, is due entirely to the dynamism of Philip Contini, managing director of the firm.

These newcomers have made Edinburgh a more exciting place than ever before in which to buy and enjoy fine wines. They have made it even harder for traditionalist merchants, like Justerini and Brooks, who, in spite of the massive backing of IDV, sumptuous premises in George Street and an excellent (and not overpriced) list, still find it hard to acquire the share of the retail trade they would regard as their due.

We live increasingly in an age of specialism, and the latest expression of this in the capital's wine scene is to be found at Davidson's Mains, where Paul Sanderson sells a unique and brilliant selection of Spanish wines.

Outside Edinburgh this specialism is less obvious, but interesting shops are beginning to appear in slightly unlikely places. Aberdeen and St Andrews have no wine merchants of note, Dundee has but one (Aitken's, on the Perth Road), and the once formidable Perth triumvirate of R. B. Smith, Matthew Gloag and Peter Thomson are no longer influential in the retail wine trade. Adventurous young merchants are, however, to be found in Peebles (Villeneuve Wines),

Lochgilphead (Marcus Fyffe Fine Wines) and Banchory, where Ian Baird has built up a modest list of interesting, if not always exceptional, 'organic' wines.

Anyone who understands the making of wine will know that this 'organic' label is far from being the ecological breakthrough it is made out to be. No-one can make wine in France, for instance, without using Bordeaux mixture (copper sulphate) as a fungicide, and all white wines need a little sulphur, while the finest of wines are always made with natural fertilisers. Still, it is to be hoped that his enterprise, and that of Edinburgh's Real Foods, who also stock the wines (Charlotte Mitchell, the owner, has written a book in praise of organic wine), will be amply rewarded.

Restaurant Wines of Distinction

Scotland boasts a handful of truly outstanding restaurant wine lists. Curiously, none of this elite group is in Edinburgh, though Martin's Restaurant in Rose Street Lane, with wines from Zubair Mohammed, is threatening to join them. The top three of these restaurants have the sorts of wine lists which draw wine lovers from all over the country – and even from overseas. Two are near our greatest golf courses, which must help. At Peat Inn, near St Andrews, David Wilson has for many years had a wine list which reflected his passion for white burgundy and claret in particular, with wines carefully laid down by himself and brought out only when ready to drink, at very modest prices indeed.

On the other side of the Forth, at Gullane, David Brown shows the same attitude as David Wilson.One comes away from both with the feeling that making money is only of secondary importance to them: first and foremost their aim is to provide the very highest quality of experience possible to their customers. La Potinière, David and Hilary Brown's charming little restaurant, is almost impossible to get into except at lunchtime on weekdays, but the wait is worthwhile. The list is remarkable for the range of old wines available, and especially in the burgundy section where there are superb wines from the 1960s and early 70s which make it almost impossible to choose.

When Houston House, a magnificent Scottish baronial house at Uphall, in West Lothian, now reborn as an elegant hotel, was run by the Knight family, it was renowned for its wine list but not taken very seriously for its food. Now it has been taken over by the group which runs Gleddoch House Hotel at Langbank, to the west of Glasgow, and though the wine list is not quite so exciting as it used to be, the food is becoming increasingly interesting. And to say that the wine list is not quite what it was is hardly an insult, considering the treasures it once held – and still does. Better still, the same sort of list has been built up at Gleddoch House, a very comfortable hotel with its own fine golf course and country club.

The most idiosyncratic restaurant wine list in Scotland must surely be that of Champany, an attractive but quirky restaurant near Linlithgow. Clive Davidson, the owner and chef, is a South African who both loves and understands beef. Perfectly hung steaks are cooked to perfection over a charcoal fire, and served simply but copiously with traditional accompaniments. The wines of Davidson's native land do figure on the wine list, but his abiding passion is for the wines of Burgundy, of which there must be hundreds in a list the size of a bad novel. Strangely, the wines are mostly too young to give maximum pleasure and the list is so compendious as to be quite unmanageable on a single visit, but it is certainly a testament to enthusiasm.

In addition to these few restaurants of distinction, there are other hotels with fine wine lists, such as the top class Inverlochy Castle. A gastronomic tour round Scotland will no doubt reveal some more.

The changing face of Crabbie's. Original ledgers, labels and bottles can be seen at the visitors' centre in Leith.

(Della Matheson)

Raisins are steeped for a week at Crabbie's to begin the winemaking process. The raisin water is fermented after steeping and forms the base for Green Ginger Wine.
(Della Matheson)

Wine Production in Scotland

Not all wine in Scotland is imported. A traditionally important element in the Scottish wine trade was the grocer who made his own wines in the back room of his grocery shop, and there are still a few indigenous wines which have a steady following.

Crabbie's Green Ginger Wine has been made at the same premises in Leith since John Crabbie moved his grocery wine trade to Great Junction Street in 1801. The secret recipe came with Crabbie to Edinburgh – legend has it, from the Highlands, when a fugitive

'John MacRabbie' was forced to flee and change his name after the Forty-Five. The business prospered and until the 1950s Crabbie's produced a range of beverages, including orange gin and peppermint cordial. They then decided to concentrate on Green Ginger Wine, their best seller, and this is now widely known simply as 'Crabbie's'. A family firm until 1964, Crabbie's is now part of United Distillers, and bottles whisky as well as making wine. Visitors are welcomed during the summer and the excellent guided tours show a working winery where much has remained traditional while meeting a modern high demand.

A bottle of Crabbie's is a blend of five wines, all of which are made in the Leith winery. The first step is to produce a base blend wine by steeping raisins in warm water for a week, during which time several quantities of water will be drawn through for fermentation. The largest fermentation vat at Crabbie's is built into the wall space, and is lined with ebon, a kind of asphalt. It holds 91 000 litres (20 000) gallons of raisin water. Fermentation proceeds for six weeks, after which the liquid is piped into oak vats and left to settle for a further three weeks. The wine then matures for a total of three years in large oak maturation vats. There are around a quarter of a million litres (165 000 gallons) of wine maturing at Crabbie's at any one time.

After two and a half years, a percentage of this base blend wine is drawn off and flavoured to form the other wines which make up the Green Ginger blend. Lemon peel wine and orangette wine use citrus fruits from the Mediterranean for flavouring, while the spiced wine is flavoured with cloves and cinnamon sticks. Cowslip wine was easy to make in Scotland at one time, but now the flowers are protected and the necessary quantities have to be imported from Eastern Europe. Elderflowers are also imported to make the elderflower wine. Once the flavouring is complete the five wines are returned to vats to complete their maturation.

The five wines plus the base wine are blended proportionately according to John Crabbie's secret recipe. An expert nosing panel checks the quality of the blend and recommends any adjustments. When the panel is satisfied, the unique ginger compound is added. This is prepared by steeping root ginger in a high strength molasses spirit, and it boosts the alcohol content as well as flavouring the blend.

The blend is stored for a short time until it has been tested by the Customs and Excise inspectors. Sugar and water are added to reduce the alcohol content to the required level before the finished wine is bottled. If the colour varies slightly, caramel will be added to give the characteristic green tinge.

Crabbie's export their Green Ginger Wine all over the world. It has a robust quality which makes it a good drink in its own right, with a very distinctive flavour. It also makes a good mixer; the well-known warming drink 'whisky mac' is made from equal measures of Crabbie's and whisky, and it is excellent in hot winter punch or mulled wine.

No discussion of wine in Scotland would be complete without a mention of the unique range of country wines produced at Moniack Castle near Inverness. The castle itself has been a seat of the Frasers since 1580, and Philippa Fraser has restored the house as well as creating the winery. It is not a small concern by any means, and as well as a steadily increasing output of wines and liqueurs, going to shops and restaurants all over Scotland and the north of England, they have lately introduced a range of preserves.

Moniack produces three white wines, one red and one rosé. The elderflower is a still and dryish white, the silver birch is drier still, and the meadowsweet is a medium sweet white with a curious constituent – natural aspirin! The full-bodied, dry red is made from blaeberries, and the most recent addition is a sweet raspberry rosé. All of the flowers and fruits are collected locally using casual labour. The silver birch, however, is made from the sap, which is tapped in spring without damage to the trees.

All of the wines are made by adding granulated sugar and German dried yeast. The fibreglass fermentation vats hold 200 litres, and after four to five weeks of fermentation at a constant 72°F the wines are transferred to 600 gallon vats (2400 litres), where they are left to

Every bottle of Crabbie's is a blend of five wines and a selection of exotic ingredients, including cinnamon, lemon peel, cowslips and elderflowers.
(Della Matheson)

Nosing panels check the quality of the blend and recommend any adjustments.

(Della Matheson)

Harvesting elderflowers for the winery at Moniack Castle.

(Michael Siebert)

mature for a year. The wines are bottled at around 14 months, after passage through a fine filter.

Each bottle of wine attracts 75 pence in duty, and they are therefore not cheap. The question, of course, is whether they can bear comparison with 'real' wines made from grapes. They taste different, and perhaps appeal more to those reared on such wines than to palates attuned to the flavour of the grape. Nevertheless, it is an enterprise which deserves to succeed, and to this end the recent opening of a visitor centre and restaurant will surely help.

Already Moniack is attracting 55 000 visitors a year, each guest being offered a talk and a tour of the winery, as well as a free tasting.

The changes in the past decade have been quite unparalleled in historical terms, to such an extent that we now live in what many wine lovers would consider the most exciting country in the world. It is not so much in spite of the fact that the grape will not grow here, but because of it, that we appreciate its fermented juice to the extent that we do.

Opposite: Much is done by hand at Moniack. Meadowsweet is measured for adding to the vats (top left); the filter is connected (top right); and the wine is bottled and corked, ready for labelling (bottom).
(Michael Siebert)

Below: Visitors to the winery are free to taste the finished product.
(Michael Siebert)

1. H. W. Thompson, quoted in Billy Kay and Cailean Maclean, *Knee Deep in Claret*, Mainstream Publishing, 1983.
2. John Home.

3. Beer – A Proud Tradition

'Did you ever taste beer?' 'I had a sip of it once,' said the small servant. 'Here's a state of things!' cried Mr Swiveller . . . 'She *never* tasted it – it can't be tasted in a sip!'[1]

Scotland, though thought of as a distilling nation, is very rich in brewing history, with a tradition which stretches back well beyond that of whisky distilling. Brewing has bequeathed a substantial legacy in terms of cultural heritage and physical remains in many locations throughout the length and breadth of the country and ale has been a recurrent theme for Scotland's literary giants, including Burns, Fergusson, Scott and Stevenson. Yet, surprisingly, little attention has been paid to the significance of brewing as an industry in Scotland, both nationally and regionally – particularly in terms of its links with other industries such as agriculture (barley cultivation), glass manufacture (bottles), sugar boiling (brewing), and coal-mining (for heating purposes). Little attempt has been made to study the brewing industry in a purely Scottish context, and apart from passing references in general works and a handful of individual company histories (often privately published and difficult to acquire), very little of note has appeared that has been devoted exclusively to the subject.

Scotland is fortunate in having plentiful supplies of those ingredients which have justifiably made its whisky so renowned, namely good water and barley. These are also vital ingredients in the brewing process. The art of brewing is reputed to have originated in Mesopotamia in about 4000 BC, and within a couple of millennia to have spread to continental Europe and to Britain. In Scotland itself, it is known that even in pre-Roman times the indigenous population made a crude form of ale from fermented grain, using darnel (corn weed) or bigg (coarse barley), with the addition of other ingredients such as rowan berries, heather shoots, broom, spruce or bog myrtle. Indeed, the Picts were reputed to be noted brewers of spruce and heather beers, as described by Robert Louis Stevenson in his nineteenth century poem, 'Heather Ale'.

> From the bonny bells of heather
> They brewed a drink langsyne
> Was sweeter far than honey
> Was stronger far than wine[2]

Although beers of this type were said to have been brewed in some outlying areas of Scotland such as Galloway, Orkney and Moray until perhaps as late as the nineteenth century, it is generally thought

Opposite: Wort is drawn through an 18-tap run-off on its way to the brewing copper.

(Alloa Brewery Company Limited)

45

Brewers' cart and dray horse 'Prince' at William Younger's Brewery in Edinburgh, around 1880.
(Scottish Brewing Archive)

that the secret of the Pictish art of brewing died out long before.

Marian McNeill, author of *The Scots Cellar*, states[3] that the Pictish mode of brewing was gradually superseded from the twelfth century onwards by the German method of brewing, the latter being very much akin to that which we know today. This method was originally brought to Britain from the Continent by religious orders. In Scotland the German method of brewing was taken up by monastic establishments at such places as Banff, Holyrood, Arbroath, Melrose and Newbattle, and remained for several centuries the exclusive preserve of the clergy. However, by the early fifteenth century the secularisation of brewing had taken place, and brewing was fairly extensively practised as a domestically based by-product of the agrarian economy. In Scotland at this time cognisance of the 'broustaris' (brewers) as they were then known, was taken in the *Leges Burgorum*, a code of burgh laws, which imposed a licence duty of four Scots pence a year on all persons engaged in brewing.[4]

While most brewers would only brew sufficient ale to meet the needs of their immediate families, from the fifteenth century onwards 'publick' breweries (who sold commercially) began to make an appearance. Possibly the first recorded brewery of this type in Scotland was established at Blackford in Perthshire, for it is known that while returning from his Coronation at Scone Palace in 1488, King James IV stopped at Blackford to purchase a barrel of ale for twelve Scots shillings.[5]

Nevertheless, for several centuries to follow, brewing remained a domestically-based occupation geared to the agrarian cycle and seasonal in nature. The brewing season was from October to March, and followed on from the harvest, with brewing being extensively practised by women in the home.

However, by the sixteenth century, in the larger towns at least, the beginnings of a formal business structure in brewing began to be discernible. A powerful Society of Brewers was established in Edinburgh as early as 1596, controlling all aspects of the brewing process from the supply of good brewing water to the purchase and malting of barley.[6] Public breweries soon became established in other early industrial centres such as Bo'ness, Glasgow, Stirling, Leith and Ayr, but generally, due to burghal and craft restrictions, their growth was slow.

As late as 1700, domestic brewing was still overwhelmingly dominant. In that year the Excise Returns show us that the County of Fife had no less than 522 brewers, of which 70 were in St Andrews alone![7] Over the next half-century, however, the growth of market forces as a result of population growth, urbanisation, and the rise of the wage economy created a level of demand which led to the establishment of many public breweries. A number of these firms were to become famous and revered names in Scottish brewing: Archibald Campbell (1710) and William Younger (1749) in Edinburgh; George Younger (1762) in Alloa, and Hugh and Robert Tennent (1740) in Glasgow, were amongst the firms established in the first half of the eighteenth century. The latter part of the eighteenth and early part of the nineteenth centuries saw the crumbling of the old burghal restrictions, and the establishment of public breweries in most towns of any size in Scotland, perhaps with the exception of the north-west. By 1850 even fairly modest towns such as Nairn, Cupar or Peebles

By 1900 Edinburgh was Scotland's main brewing centre. Staff at William Younger's at the end of the nineteenth century.

(Scottish Brewing Archive)

William Younger's Holyrood Brewery in the 1930s. When brewing ceased there in 1986 it was the first time for nearly 800 years that no brewing had been undertaken on the site.
(Scottish Brewing Archive)

could boast of several breweries each. Internal transport was as yet poor, so that many of the breweries tended to be situated adjacent to barley-growing areas, or on the coast where they could easily be supplied with raw materials by sea. Outwith the burgeoning urban areas, most of these breweries tended to be small, and served strictly local markets using strictly local practices to produce their own distinctive malts and ales. Although not necessarily situated in exclusively rural areas, these breweries, to distinguish them from their larger urban counterparts, were always known thereafter as the 'country breweries'.

Taken overall, the indigenous Scottish market for ale was small and poor during the eighteenth century, and from the mid-century onwards a proportion of the output was always exported, principally to England, but also to the Low Countries and the Baltic States, and to Scottish expatriates in the Americas and the West Indies. In the nineteenth century, with Scots often being at the forefront of imperial expansion, new export markets in India, Australia and the Far East were presenting themselves. Due to the strength and quality of her ales Scotland was well placed to take advantage of these markets.

Domestically, the situation changed after 1850, with improved internal transport facilities due to the coming of the railways. This exposed many of the small country brewers to the full force of competition from their larger urban counterparts whose size conferred on them the cost benefits of economies of scale. As a result, many of the country breweries succumbed, some, such as the one at Biggar, almost immediately. A trend towards rationalisation and consolidation towards larger units began which has continued down to the present day. Although demand continued to rise, the total number of breweries, having reached a peak of about 280 in 1840, began to decline thereafter.[8]

By the turn of the twentieth century the brewing industry in Scotland had become heavily concentrated in the central lowlands, in particular in three main areas, Edinburgh, Glasgow and Alloa. Edinburgh, for so long the pre-eminent Scottish brewing city, was by far the main centre, with some 35 breweries in all. The excellent supply of hard water, eminently suitable for the brewing of pale ales, then in demand at home and abroad, contributed to Edinburgh's popularity as a centre. Alloa had eight breweries in 1900, and was similarly endowed with good water from the Ochil Hills. Alloa Ale too had an enviable reputation, as evinced by this eulogy written in 1827 by John Imlah:

Alloa Ale

Awa' wi black brandy, red rum, and blue whisky
    An' bring me the liquor as brown as a nut;
O! Alloa Ale ye can mak a chiel frisky,
    Brisk, faeming a' fresh frae the bottle or butt.
An awa wi' your wines – they are dull as moss water,
    Wi' blude colour'd blushes, or purple, or pale;
Guid folks gif ye wish to get fairer and fatter,
    Then aye weet your seasans wi' Alloa Ale!

Gif ye wish healthie habits an' wad be lang livers,
    Then spirituous drinks ye s'oud never fash wi';
But Alloa Ale ye may drink it in rivers,
    An' the deeper ye drink, aye the better ye'll be,
Sae potent as physic its virtues are valued,
    They daily wha drink look hearty an' hale;
O ye a' hae heard tell o' a Balm got in Gilead,
    Tak my word for't twas neathing but Alloa Ale!

Then countrymen croud roun' the bizzing ale bicker,
    An waur no on whisky your siller an' sense;
Nae gate ye'll fa' in wi' the like o' this liquor,
    That thro' body an saul can sic vigour dispense.
Let nae Brandy-bibber scare you wi' his scoffin,
    At prudence in drink – till he tire lat him rail;
Ilk a dram that he drinks is a nail in his coffin,
    But you'll lenthen your life-lease wi' Alloa Ale.[9]

Glasgow, with its soft water, was primarily a centre for the brewing of stout and porter, and had some 14 breweries at the turn of the century. Other major breweries were situated in Perth, Dundee and Falkirk.

By this time Scottish beer was exported worldwide, to Africa, Malaya, Burma, New Zealand, India and every outpost of the Empire, although some of the older markets in the Americas and the West Indies were in long-term decline. The Scottish brewing industry was heavily dependent on its export and military markets, and from the third quarter of the nineteenth century to the outbreak of the Second World War, Scotland accounted for at least one-quarter of all beer exported from the United Kingdom.[10] Nearer to home, the north-east of England was a very big market for Scottish ales and beers, although already the spread of the tied-house system in England was beginning to affect adversely the trade that Scottish brewers conducted there. As

During the First and Second World Wars many brewery jobs were taken over by women. Here female workers clean out the large vat at Wellpark Brewery in Glasgow.
(Scottish Brewing Archive)

*On the production line
women check bottles and
pack beer crates.*

(Scottish Brewing Archive)

a result, in order to safeguard these outlets, some Scottish brewery companies, such as Aitchisons of Edinburgh and Youngers of Alloa, acquired breweries in the north-east of England, primarily for their tied houses.

The First World War, with its commodity and output restrictions, hit many Scottish brewers hard. The Glasgow breweries, for example, relying as they did to a large extent on stout and porter brewing which required a great deal of hops and sugar, were all but decimated. Of the 92 breweries operating in Scotland in 1910, only 63 survived to 1920,[11] a virtual one-in-three casualty rate over a single decade. Another threat was posed by the Temperance Movement, which was very strong in Scotland in the years leading up to the First World War. Following the relative failure of the 1920 Local Veto Option Polls, however, the Temperance Movement went into long-term decline, although it continued to remain a powerful force in Scotland until after the Second World War.

From 1920, following a brief post-war boom, a slump ensued which lasted until the outbreak of the Second World War. The number of breweries was further reduced until only 36 remained by 1940.[12] The Second World War had an even more traumatic effect on the industry in Scotland than the previous War. Many overseas markets were lost (for ever as it happened) with the result that with its heavy dependence on the export trade, the Scottish brewing industry suffered severely. In the post-war years, this was further compounded by falling beer sales. The advent of television meant that more people stayed at home, and fewer people went out to the public house. Pubs ceased to fulfil the same social function as in pre-war days. As a result, by the post-war years there was substantial over-capacity in the industry in Scotland. Nevertheless, some small breweries serving essentially local markets survived the Second World War in towns such as Dalkeith, Cambus, Musselburgh, Laurencekirk, Dumbarton and Dunbar.

In the 1950s, there were numerous attempts to achieve some measure of rationalisation of the industry in Scotland, by forming a Scottish-based consortium of the smaller independent brewers. These moves came to nought, however, leaving the breweries ripe for picking off one-by-one by larger combines, mainly based south of the border. 1960 was the *annus-terribilis* in Scottish brewery history. There were still 26 breweries in Scotland, of which 17 were in Edinburgh alone,[13] but that year, no less than ten independent Scottish breweries were swallowed up by larger combines. These included some of the most famous names in Scottish brewing history, such as Aitken, Bernard, Fowler, Jeffrey, Murray, Morison, Maclachlan, Robert Younger, and George Younger. Most were to close within a few years, and the total number of breweries was more than halved within ten years, leaving only eleven breweries in

A modern brewery with a space age look.
(Scottish & Newcastle Breweries plc)

Left: Malted barley and water are mixed in the Lauter tun to extract the wort which is fermented.
(Alloa Brewery Company Limited)

1970.[14] By 1989 this had been further reduced to seven breweries, of which only three, Belhaven of Dunbar (estd 1719), Maclays of Alloa (estd 1830) and the Caledonian Brewing Company of Edinburgh (estd 1869), can now be considered to be nominally independent. In addition there is one large Scottish-based consortium, Scottish & Newcastle Breweries Ltd, formed from a merger of Wm Younger (estd 1749) and McEwans (estd 1856) along with sundry other companies, which recently beat off a take-over bid from a foreign predator. The remaining companies in Scotland, Tennents (estd 1740) which operates breweries in both Edinburgh and Glasgow, and Alloa Brewery Co. of Alloa (estd 1810), are both subsidiaries of English-based concerns. A measure of the decline of the Scottish brewing tradition can be gauged from the fact that when brewing

The degree of kilning which arrests the barley's germination results in pale (bottom left), amber or dark (bottom right) malts.
(Alloa Brewery Company Limited)

53

Women roll out the barrels at Wellpark Brewery in Glasgow during World War I.

(Scottish Brewing Archive)

ceased at the Holyrood brewery in Edinburgh's Canongate in May 1986, it was the first time in nearly 800 years that no brewing had been undertaken on this site.

The Brewing Process

The basics of the brewing process have remained largely unchanged over the centuries. The brewing of ale and beer quite simply involves the use of a large volume of liquid (water) to which quantities of solids (malt, hops, sugar, etc.) are added at various stages of the process.

Next to water, the chief raw ingredient in brewing is barley. This is steeped in water and then allowed to germinate, which frees the starch in the barley. At a certain stage in the germination process, this is arrested by kilning, the degree of kilning variously producing pale, amber or dark malts. The resulting malted barley is stored in malt-bins to mature, and then is milled in order to crack open (but not to grind) the malted barley kernel. This is mashed or sparged in hot water, which releases fermentable sugars resulting in a liquid extract of malt known as wort. The wort is filtered and transferred to the brewing copper where it is boiled with hops, which add flavour and convey aromatic and preservative properties. The hopped wort is then fed through a hopback (nowadays more likely a centrifuge) to remove the hops, and then is cooled and goes into the fermenting vessels, where yeast is added and the fermentation process takes place, producing ethanol (ethyl alcohol) and carbon dioxide. The yeast is then skimmed off, and the resultant beverage – beer – is drained off for maturation, either in casks or conditioning vessels.

Although the equipment in breweries is nowadays increasingly sophisticated, the same biochemical changes take place in the production of the beers as centuries ago, although in earlier times the precise nature of these changes was little understood.

The first stage in the brewing process is the malting of the barley. Traditionally, most Scottish brewers were also maltsters, and through malting the brewing industry in Scotland had very important links with agriculture. Many early brewers were farmers or landowners seeking an outlet for either their surplus crops or capital. For example, in the eighteenth century the Tennent family farmed an area north of Glasgow known as Easter Common, on which they grew barley to supply to their brewery at Wellpark. Much Scottish ale in the seventeenth and eighteenth centuries was notoriously poor, due largely to the poor quality of the barley grown in many areas, and much ale was imported from England. In 1625, however, the Scottish Parliament banned the sale of imported English ale, although this ban seems to have been widely evaded. The traditional Scottish barley was 'bear' or 'bigg', a coarse, hardy barley which could be grown on marginal land and had a short ripening season, but it was not suitable for brewing, needing prolonged steeping and mashing due to its thick husk. Following the Act of Union, however, agricultural improvement spread to Scotland, and a superior two-rowed 'common' barley was introduced, which prospered well in the fertile, agricultural areas such as East Lothian, Fife, Angus and Buchan. However, top quality English barley was always much in demand, especially that from East Anglia, which was shipped up the east coast to supply the larger breweries in places such as Edinburgh and Alloa.

Large quantities of beer mature in huge vats in the modern brewery.
(Scottish & Newcastle Breweries plc)

55

In the brewhouse the wort is boiled with hops in brewing coppers, which are distinctly different from the copper whisky stills.

(Alloa Brewing Company Limited)

Traditionally, two main types of ale were produced in Scotland. The pre-eminent drink was a strong dark sweet heavy ale known simply as 'Scotch Ale'. This was the drink of the upper classes, although many of the gentry and nobility preferred wine and in particular, claret, which was readily available in Scotland. The other popular beer, much in demand amongst the lower classes (indeed, the bulk of the population) was 'small' or table beer, universally known as 'Tuppenny' from its price per Scots pint at the time of the Act of Union, under an article of which (Article VIII) it was expressly protected from high taxation.[15] This beer was a by-product of the strong ale in that it was a result of a second mashing (or sparging) of the spent grains. A Captain Burt, an English officer engaged in superintending General Wade's road-making work, gave an account of 'Tuppeny' as sold in the Highlands:

> The liquor is disagreeable to those who are not used to it; . . . the malt, which is dried with peat, turf, or furzes, gives to a drink a taste of that kind of fuel; . . . the drink itself is apt to give a diarrhoea . . .[16]

Another popular drink that spread to Scotland by the late eighteenth century was porter. Originally porter was brought up from England, where the drink had been conceived, but having become a popular drink amongst the growing artisan classes, porter brewing was introduced to Scotland, and quickly became established in Glasgow in particular. Porter was brewed with the addition of dark malt, roasted barley, and a good deal of sugar and hops, and then was allowed to mature for months until sufficiently mellowed. Porter maintained its popularity as a drink throughout the nineteenth and into the twentieth century, being gradually superseded by pale ales.

Until the latter part of the nineteenth century, brewing was still a seasonal occupation, lasting from October to March or April. In these latter months strong 'keeping' beers were brewed and laid down, beers whose strength would allow them to last through the summer months. The strength of these beers also allowed them to survive in hot climates, and from the mid-eighteenth century onwards strong Scotch Ales were being exported in small quantities to overseas destinations, notably to the West Indies where there was a colony of Scots expatriates. Probably because there was insufficient demand to constitute a whole cargo, a hogshead or two would be despatched as part of a general cargo. Beers for more immediate and domestic sale were known as 'running beers', and for them, climatic and seasonal variations were of less importance. By the mid-nineteenth century the larger breweries in urban areas with good markets and a steady turn-over were already practising all-the-year-round brewing.

Scottish brewing practice was distinctive, and departed from English practice in several important respects. Writing in 1837, W. H. Roberts in his book *The Scottish Ale Brewer and Practical Maltster* remarked on these differences, notably that mashing took place at a higher temperature, and the resultant wort was fermented much longer (about 21 days), at lower temperatures (10°C). Also, sparging was a Scottish innovation, as opposed to subsequent mashing as in England.[17]

In addition to cask beer, bottled beer was available from the major breweries, either in stone or glass bottles, although this was something of a luxury trade, as there was an excise duty on glass manufacture between 1745 and 1845. Beer for bottling had to be

*A cooper's workshop
at McEwan's Fountain
Brewery.*
(Scottish Brewing Archive)

matured until sufficiently flattened, that is, until the fermentation
had worked its way out, and this might take many months. Before
the scientific appraisal of brewing took place in the late nineteenth
century, the bottling of beer was something of a speculative business,
the resulting product frequently ranging in character from the flat to
the explosive.

Towards the latter part of the nineteenth century Scottish brewers, particularly those in the east, turned increasingly towards the
production of lower gravity highly hopped beers, which became
known as Pale Ales. Hops had traditionally been used somewhat
sparingly in Scotland, primarily for simple economic reasons, and
these beers were in colour and flavour a departure from traditional
Scotch Ales. Their prime attraction to the brewers lay in the fact that
they had a shorter fermentation period and a quicker turnover, and
despite their lower gravity, their high hop content ensured that they
travelled well and retained their clarity in hot climates. Whilst these
beers proved eminently suitable for export markets, they also found
ready acceptance on the domestic market, where the water supply
was still far from perfect in many towns, and where light beers

formed part of many people's general diet. Those beers which were exported to the Colonies became known as 'India' Pale Ales.

Another late nineteenth century innovation was lager beer. This had been imported into the country from Germany and Denmark in small but increasing quantities in the latter part of the nineteenth century, and was on sale in many of the better class licensed grocers' shops in the major cities. Tennents of Glasgow commenced brewing lager in a small way in 1885, and such was the success of the venture that they constructed a complete lager brewery in 1890, importing German brewers and coopers expressly for this purpose. Using special lager malts (pale, lightly kilned malts), bottom-fermenting yeast strains, low temperature (8°C) fermentations and protracted conditioning by lagering (i.e. cold storing) at very low temperatures for several months, then filtering and pasteurising in the bottle, they produced a pale, sparkling, light drink which won ready acceptance, both at home and abroad. Tennents' venture into lager brewing was successful enough for a number of other Scottish brewers to follow suit, notably Jeffreys of Edinburgh and Arrols of Alloa.

Pasteurisation was another great breakthrough in the latter part of the nineteenth century. The pioneering research of scientists like Louis Pasteur, coupled with technical developments such as the advent of steam power and refrigeration, made all-the-year-round brewing feasible for most breweries.

By the turn of the twentieth century, the older Scottish beers – strong ale, table beers, and porter – although continuing to be

Bottling beer and packing crates at McEwan's Fountain Brewery.
(Scottish Brewing Archive)

An intriguing beer bottle design from the mid-thirties, which was soon withdrawn because of the resemblance to bottles of household cleaner.

(Scottish Brewing Archive)

produced, had declined in comparison to pale and mild ales and stout. Most Scottish brewers at this time produced a wide range of beers of varying strength, colours and qualities. The traditional method of categorising Scottish beers, at least from 1880 when Beer Duty replaced Sugar and Malt Tax, was by way of the 'shilling terminology'. Under this system, beers were categorised by price per barrel in order of ascending strength. Most breweries produced beers ranging from very weak Table and Harvest beers of 28/– and 36/–, Light and Mild Beers of 42/– and 48/–, Pale Ales of 54/– and 60/–, Export and Imperial ales of 70/– and 80/–, right up to Strong Ales of Twelve and Fifteen Guineas, on top of which a range of stouts and porters would be brewed. The ales at the strongest end of the range were very potent, and were usually sold in bottle form in 'nips' of $\frac{1}{3}$ imperial pint. 'Nips' were known as 'Wee Heavy' beers, a term peculiar to Scotland, as indeed was the whole shilling terminology itself. It must be stressed that the shilling system was only an invoice price, the real price being determined by taking into account both beer duty and discounts offered by the brewers, which in some cases could be substantial, amounting to as much as 50 per cent of the cost of a barrel. Hence the invoice price was only an indication of the type of beer, the real price being determined by the size and amount of the discount and duties. To further complicate matters, this terminology was applied not only to barrels of 36 gallons, but also to hogsheads of 54 gallons and sometimes to larger containers also. Thus what in barrel was 60/– Ale, became in hogshead 90/– Ale, although this was exactly the same beer.

The shilling terminology continued in Scotland long after the terms ceased to serve any useful purpose, beyond roughly indicating the type and strength of the beers that it represented. After the Second

World War, with the range of beers having shrunk considerably, a shilling system was gradually superseded by the terms Light, Heavy and Export. Light was a low gravity beer, the successor to Mild. Perversely, it was usually darker in colour. Heavy was a medium gravity sweeter beer which came into vogue from the 1940s and was really a strong pale mild ale. Export and IPA (India Pale Ale) were superior quality beers, stronger and darker than heavy. As their names suggest, they had originally been brewed for the export market. In addition there was stout, a more bitter derivative of porter. Stout was complemented post-Second World War by Sweet Stout, which was often a concoction of other beers. Another fairly recent introduction has been Special, a carbonated, pasteurised version of Heavy. The terms Light, Heavy, Special, Export and 'Wee Heavy' are predominantly although not exclusively Scottish, and these beers have no real equivalents south of the border.

Of the older Scottish beers, table beer and porter have now disappeared entirely in Scotland, while stouts and strong ales, at least in bottle form, make up a small and declining sector of the market. However, Caledonian, Belhaven and Maclays all brew and market a draught strong ale which is somewhat akin to the old traditional Scotch Ale in colour and strength.

Bottled and Keg Beers

The techniques of carbonisation, pasteurisation and filtration had been introduced for bottled beers in the late nineteenth century. This process involved filtering and pasteurising the beer, then injecting it with carbonic acid gas, which produced a clear, sparkling if slightly acid beer, but one which was stable and inert and had a long shelf life. This had obvious advantages, both for export and domestic purposes, but many brewers were reluctant to attempt this process with cask beer, despite the introduction into Britain by the 1930s of metal barrels or kegs. However, the much changed trading conditions after the Second World War, with declining standards of cellarmanship and bartending, plus an embargo on the import of good quality foreign malting barley, hastened the introduction of this type of beer in bulk. It was known as keg beer.

The trend towards a 'convenience beer' simply mirrored the trend towards convenience foodstuffs in the food industry, and although such a beer had many attractions at the time, both for brewer and publican alike, something of a reaction set in during the late 1970s and the 1980s. This period witnessed the establishment of more than a dozen new small breweries in Scotland, dedicated to producing beer on a small scale in a traditional manner. Although many of these breweries proved short-lived, in size of output and even in types of product they are more reminiscent of the small breweries of previous

Right: A calendar for William Younger's from 1910. Advertising took off in the brewing industry in the early part of the twentieth century.

(Scottish Brewing Archive)

Opposite: The modern production line – kegging at speed.

(Alloa Brewery Company Limited)

centuries. One of these breweries actually produced a porter, so the wheel turned full circle.

In terms of the numbers of remaining breweries, the industry in Scotland is very small compared with that of previous times. Total capacity and output is, however, much greater than ever

Right: Metal kegs stacked in the warehouse.
(Scottish & Newcastle Breweries plc)

Below: The face of modern bulk brewing, with processes monitored and controlled at the computer.
(Scottish & Newcastle Breweries plc)

before as modern modes of production allow a much greater output of beer to be produced by fewer breweries. Only seven major breweries survive in Scotland in addition to a handful of very small 'micro-breweries'.

The Scottish market is largely controlled by Tennent Caledonian and Scottish & Newcastle who between them account for some 80 per cent of all indigenous beer sales. Tennents have long been Scotland's pre-eminent lager brewers, but have also made inroads in recent years into the ale market, while conversely Scottish & Newcastle have had some success in gaining a share of the lager market. Scottish & Newcastle, with their registered offices in Edinburgh, are now nominally Scotland's largest manufacturing company, yet they have only one brewery remaining in Scotland, compared with no less than five in England.

Alloa Brewery Company, a subsidiary of the English giant, Allied-Lyons, is Scotland's third biggest brewing company – it brews both ales and lager – and has in recent years swallowed the businesses and tied estates of two other long-established Scottish brewing concerns, Ushers and Drybroughs. Alloa can boast another long-established brewery firm too, that of Maclay & Co. Ltd, whose fine traditional tower brewery (the Thistle Brewery) is a notable local landmark. Maclays eschew the brewing of lager altogether, preferring instead

Traquair House, home of the highly distinctive Traquair House Ales and Traquair Bear Ales.
(Peter Maxwell-Stewart of Traquair)

to concentrate wholeheartedly on a range of traditional Scottish ales. Their Edinburgh counterparts, the Caledonian Brewery Company, also produce only ales from their splendid red-brick Victorian tower brewery.

Finally, at Belhaven near Dunbar can be found Scotland's oldest extant brewery, the Belhaven Brewery, which now produces lager as well as traditional ales in a delightfully rural setting. It is possible to visit all those breweries in organised parties by prior arrangement.

Another Scottish brewery which deserves special mention is Traquair House, near Innerleithen in the Scottish Borders. Reputedly the oldest continually inhabited house in Scotland, the story of the brewhouse is a fascinating one. A number of years ago the present Laird of Traquair, Mr Peter Maxwell-Stewart, was cleaning out some little-used cellars when he discovered a complete eighteenth century brewhouse, which had originally supplied the house and estate workers with ale, but which had long lain unused. The brewhouse, which was thought to date from about 1720, was put back into commission in 1965, and since that time the Traquair brewhouse has continued to produce its highly distinctive ales, which can be found in both draught and bottled form in specialist outlets. The brewhouse is open to visitors, along with the house and gardens, from April to September.

The brewhouse at Traquair, thought to date from about 1720, began producing beer again in 1965.
(Peter Maxwell-Stewart of Traquair)

In some ways, despite being over two hundred years old, Traquair House can be regarded as the first of the generation of new breweries which sprang up in Scotland in the 1970s and 1980s. These breweries, which to date total some 15 in all, were established largely as a result of the 'real-ale' movement which filled a perceived gap in the market for traditional cask beers which the major companies were often accused of neglecting.

Described by some as the most successful consumer movement in post-war Britain, the movement is epitomised by the acronymic consumer pressure-group CAMRA (the Campaign for Real Ale). Dedicated to promoting unpressurised cask beers, CAMRA has had a rather more limited impact in Scotland than has its counterpart south of the border, due to the much smaller number of surviving breweries in Scotland. However, CAMRA in Scotland has been successful to the extent that all the brewery companies now offer at least one traditional cask beer, but it has not achieved the wholesale reversals of policy that it has in some parts of England. The major brewers in Scotland are still overwhelmingly committed to large-volume carbonated and pasteurised keg beers and lagers. Cask 'real-ales', although they can be found in the major centres, form only a very small percentage of the total market and many Scots seem to actually prefer carbonated beers. However, the Caledonian Brewery in Edinburgh produces nothing but cask 'real-ales', as does the small Harviestoun Brewery near Dollar, whilst cask beer forms a significant part of the total output of Belhaven, Broughton and Maclays breweries. In addition to advocating the merits of cask beers, CAMRA also organise some very popular Beer Festivals, where many types of cask beer not readily available are on offer: this has led to a growing awareness amongst the Scottish public of English regional beers, which in the major centres such as Edinburgh and Glasgow are now gaining ready acceptance, a phenomenon virtually unthinkable ten years ago.

Most of the 'new breweries' which started in response to the 'real-ale' movement have faced a hard struggle to survive as the major companies control the bulk of the outlets either directly or indirectly. Many have proved short-lived. Perhaps the best known extant new brewery is the Broughton Brewery, situated in the Peeblesshire village of that name. Their Greenmantle Ales can be found throughout Scotland in selected outlets. The aggregate output of these breweries is infinitesimal, hence they are often dubbed 'micro-breweries'.

A rather different version of the new small brewery can be found in Edinburgh. This is the Rose Street Brewery, Scotland's only example of a pub brewery. This is a modern version of a very traditional concept. At the Rose Street Brewery the entire brewing process can be viewed by the public-house customers from within the pub by way of glass viewing panels, with the finished end-product being available for sampling at the bar.

67

Methods of Dispensing

Traditionally, from the turn of the century at least, beers have been dispensed in Scotland by way of tall fonts and water-engines. Tall pillar beer fonts were until recent years a familiar feature of many Scottish pubs, allowing the pint to be poured above bar-level in full view of the customers. These tall fonts were used in conjunction with a water-engine in the cellar, which raised the beer from the cask to the font by means of air-pressure, producing a pint of beer with the tight, creamy head long favoured in Scotland. With the advent of the carbonated keg beers from the 1950s onwards, tall fonts began to disappear from many Scottish pubs, to be replaced by keg taps. In recent years, however, tall fonts have made something of a comeback, although nowadays they are served by electric compressors rather than the older water-engines.

The Scottish Pub

The Bow Bar in Edinburgh, where customers can choose from more than 25 beers.
(Della Matheson)

The traditional Scottish howff or tavern frequented by Robert Burns and his contemporaries has all but disappeared. These howffs were simply dwelling-houses with some of the rooms opened up for the

purpose of drinking. Although snug and convivial, these types of pubs were frowned on in Victorian times as dens of illicit gambling and moral degeneracy. Most were swept away under the licensing restrictions and Improvement Acts of the mid nineteenth century, to be replaced by a very different type of pub, the Victorian 'Palace Pub'. Large, open and roomy establishments, often with a central or island bar commanding the entire establishment, the 'Palace Pub' was in marked contrast to the older 'dram-shops' where it had often been difficult for the publican to supervise exactly what was going on in each of the separate rooms. The 'Palace Pubs' featured imposing gantries, sumptuous glazed tilework, elaborately carved woodwork, stained glass and etched mirrors. In addition these establishments were staffed by a small army of aproned barmen and waiters, and as such were intended to have a civilising effect on attitudes towards drink.

The public houses of late Victorian and Edwardian times are generally regarded as the apogee of pub design in Scotland, both aesthetically and architecturally. Although there are some contemporary pubs of note, no readily identifiable style has subsequently emerged on a similar scale. A relatively small number of 'Palace Pubs' have survived down to the present day but they include the magnificent Café Royal, Abbotsford, Kenilworth and Bennets Bars in Edinburgh, the Horseshoe Bar in Glasgow, the Speedwell Bar in Dundee, the Phoenix Bar in Inverness and the Grill Bar in Aberdeen. Almost unbelievably, fine examples of the style are still being destroyed and many have been unsympathetically modernised out of all recognition.

One or two splendid public houses dating from the inter-war years can also still be found. These were built as variants of the prevailing styles of the 1920s and 1930s, 'art-nouveau', 'art-deco', and 'moderne'. Public houses of this era were never constructed on any great scale in Scotland, although some generously-proportioned roadhouses were constructed on the outskirts of some of the major towns, while a handful of bijou inner-city pubs of these styles also appeared. The best surviving examples of this era are the Maybury Roadhouse on the western outskirts of Edinburgh, the Stepps Bar and Rogano's in Glasgow, and the Clep Bar in Dundee.

In the era following the Second World War, and especially during the 1960s and 1970s, pub design in Scotland reached an absolute nadir. No identifiable style appeared, and the major brewers, who controlled an ever-increasing proportion of pubs, were seemingly engaged in the systematic destruction of pubs of an earlier period while simultaneously trying to recreate a spurious type of mock-Victoriana based on flock wallpaper, chandeliers, and velour drapes. Occasionally a modern pub of some merit would slip through the net, such as Carsons Bar at Coatbridge, but these are few and far between.

Although Scotland has a long and proud tradition in brewing, this has been allowed to be obscured and neglected to some extent in recent years. At one time Scotch Ales were exported to the farthest corners of the globe and were in every way synonymous with quality. As late as the 1950s the international reputation of Scotch Ales was at least as great as that of Scotch Whisky, but in recent years that of Scotch Ales has declined relative to whisky, not because of any drop in quality, but because the proud traditions and heritage of the Scottish brewing industry have not been projected the way they might have been. This situation has been somewhat redressed by the

A selection of beer mats and labels.
(Scottish Brewing Archive)

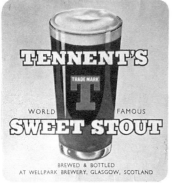

support given by the brewing industry in Scotland to the formation
... sed at
... decade
... ory of,
... is unit
... fitting
... al and

... n, 1891,

... inburgh,

... in Alloa,

... gh, 84B,

... Scottish

PLEASE NOTE: THIS LIST SUPERSEDES THE ONE GIVEN ON PAGE 71.

IT MAY BE POSSIBLE TO VISIT THE FOLLOWING BREWERIES IN ORGANISED PARTIES BY PRIOR ARRANGEMENT.

Alloa Brewery Co. Ltd, Alloa Brewery, Whins Road, Alloa, Clackmannan. Trade visits only: apply in writing to Sheila McPherson.

Alloa Brewery Co. Ltd, Rose Street Brewery, Rose Street, Edinburgh. Tel: 031 225 1660.

Belhaven Brewery Co. Ltd, Belhaven, Dunbar, East Lothian. Trade visits only: Tel: David Broadhurst, 0368 62734.

Broughton Brewery Co. Ltd, Broughton Brewery, Broughton, Biggar, Lanarkshire. Trade visits given preference. Wednesday evenings only, twenty-five maximum. Apply in writing to David Younger.

Caledonian Brewing Co. Ltd, Caledonian Brewery, Slateford Road, Edinburgh. Apply in writing to John Dawson.

Harviestoun Brewery Company, Harviestoun Brewery, Dollarfield Farm, Dollar, Clackmannan. Tel: Ken Brooker, 0259 42141.

Maclay & Co. Ltd, Thistle Brewery, East Vennel, Alloa, Clackmannan. Preference given to trade visits. Wednesday afternoons only. Tel: Duncan Kellock, 0259 723387.

Orkney Brewery Company, Quoyloo, Sandwick, Orkney. Tel: Roger Whyte, 085 684802.

Scottish & Newcastle Breweries plc, Fountain Brewery, Fountainbridge, Edinburgh. Daily, 10.15 a.m. and 2–5 p.m. Maximum of twenty. Tel: Maxine Mendelssohn, 031 229 9377.

Tennent Caledonian Breweries Ltd, Heriot Brewery, Roseburn Terrace, Edinburgh. Trade visits only. Apply in writing to Eleanor Wilson.

Tennent Caledonian Breweries Ltd, Wellpark Brewery, Duke Street, Glasgow. Trade visits only. Apply in writing to Janice Ely.

Traquair House Brewery, Traquair, Innerleithen, Peeblesshire. Tel: 0896 830323.

Belhaven Brewery, Belhaven, Dunbar, East Lothian. Tel. 0368 62734.
  Contact: Alistair Mouat.

Caledonian Brewery, Slateford Road, Edinburgh. Tel. 031 337 1286.
  Contact: John Dawson.

Alloa Brewery, Whins Road, Alloa, Clackmannan. Tel. 031 661 6161.
  Contact: Pauline Williams.

Maclean Company Ltd, Thistle Brewery, Alloa, Clackmannan. Tel. 0259 623387.
  Contact: George King.

Scottish and Newcastle Breweries, Fountain Brewery, Fountainbridge, Edinburgh. Tel. 031 229 9377.
  Contact: Maxine Mendelssohn.

Tennant Caledonian Brewery Ltd, Wellpark Brewery, Duke Street, Glasgow. Tel. 041 552 6552.
  Contact: Janice Ely.

Tennant Caledonian Brewery Ltd, Heriot Brewery, Roseburn Terrace, Edinburgh. Tel. 031 337 1361.
  Contact: Marie Sommerville.

Traquair House, Innerleithen, Peeblesshire. Tel. 0896 830323.
  Contact: Peter Maxwell Stuart.

Harvistoun Brewery, Dollar Field Farm, Harviestoun, By Dollar. Tel. 0259 42141.
  Contact: Ken Brooker.

4. Whisky – Quality of Scotland

I had companions, I had friends,
I had of whisky various blends.
The whisky was all drunk; and lo!
The friends were gone for evermo![1]

When the Scotch finally arrives in the glass after its lengthy and careful creation, it is there to be appreciated in whatever circumstances it is consumed, under a hot African sun, in the sticky heat of the Orient, in the cold and wet of a Scottish winter. There is no correct way to enjoy such a versatile drink. Some declare it ruined if it is not taken neat. Others will not touch it without water. Some advocate lemonade, others soda. Some abhor ice, while others demand it – yet all delight in Scotland's greatest ambassador.

Opposite: A maltster turns the 'piece' with a wooden shiel at Highland Park distillery in Orkney.
(Matthew Gloag & Son Limited)

Below: Cutting peat in the traditional way. Peat is cut early in the summer and stacked to dry.
(Matthew Gloag & Son Limited)

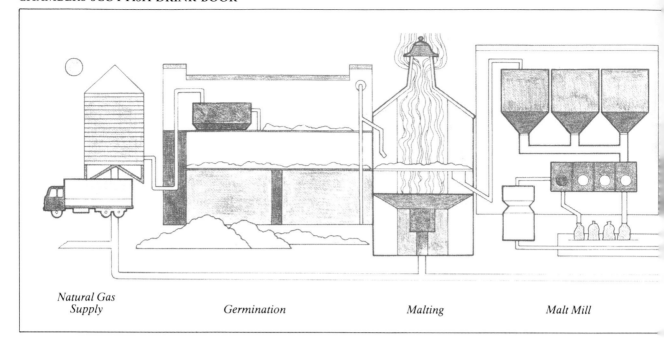

Natural Gas
Supply   Germination   Malting   Malt Mill

The Making of Scotch Whisky

The ingredients for making whisky are exactly the same as those used to make malt ales – fresh water, malted barley and yeast. The process begins in the same way. Ripened barley is germinated to convert the starches in each grain into sugars. Traditionally barley, often grown locally, was malted at the distilleries on large open malt floors. These buildings with their low ceilings, stone or tiled floors, and neat rows of small windows, can still be seen at many distilleries. Most have now been converted into whisky bonds or visitors' centres. Only a very few distilleries make malt in this way.

Among such distinguished distilleries are Bowmore on Islay and Highland Park at Kirkwall in Orkney. Here the visitor can witness a craft that extends back for centuries, certainly to the fifteenth century in Scotland. The barley is first soaked in a large vessel called a 'steep' for two to three days. It is then placed in another receptacle called a 'couch' to drain before being spread out to germinate on the malting floor to the depth of about 30 cm, when it is known as the 'piece'. To prevent the piece from heating up and the grain rotting, it must be turned regularly. This was done traditionally by using wooden ploughs and rakes to open the piece and then by tossing the grain in the air with wooden shovels, called 'shiels'. More recently, mechanical ploughs and rakes have been used for this purpose. After about a week, depending on the weather, the rootlet on the grain has grown to about twice the length of the grain and the starches have turned into sugars to feed the embryonic plant. This process, known as modification, was monitored by the simple

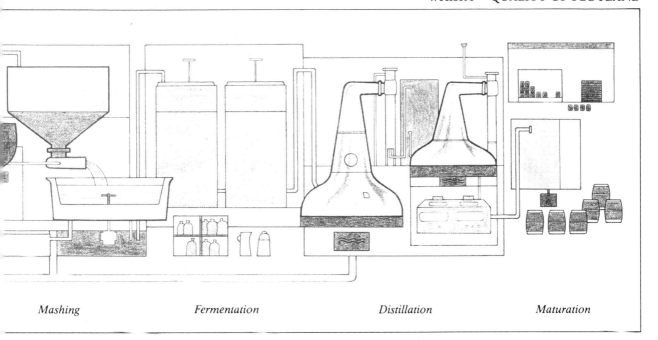

| Mashing | Fermentation | Distillation | Maturation |

Distillation processes in malt whisky.

(British Gas Scotland)

expedient of biting the grain. When the maltster judges the process to be complete, it is halted by drying the 'green malt' in a kiln.

The temperature in the kiln is raised gradually, but must not exceed 70°C to ensure that the enzyme (diastase) in the malt is not destroyed. Originally in the Highlands the malt was dried over a peat fire, but from the late eighteenth century coke or anthracite began to be used. Peat continued to be added to the fire in varying quantities to impart the characteristic reek to the malt which forms an essential ingredient in certain malt whiskies.

The remnants of kilns for drying grain are to be found in the many deserted villages scattered throughout the Highlands. They are normally made of stone and shaped like a bowl in the ground, with an arched furnace beneath. The kiln would have been covered with a simple thatch and used for drying the barley and oats grown in the township as well as malt. From about the 1750s more elaborate kilns were erected at the larger distilleries incorporating technologies developed by maltsters in England. The kilns had tapering roofs to draw the heat from the furnace through the drying floor on which the malt was laid out. This was constructed either of very fine wire mesh or perforated tiles, manufactured mostly in East Anglia. The kilns were capped with horizontal ventilators, often designed to look like the roofs of Chinese pagodas. Many distilleries have preserved their malt kilns, even if they have been converted to other purposes, because they are salient features in the landscapes. Up and down the east coast of Britain old malt kilns can be seen piercing the skyline, notably at the famous Snape Maltings concert hall in Suffolk. When the malt has been dried, the rootlets, 'culms', are cleaned off in

Adding peat to the furnace beneath a traditional malt kiln. Peat gives some malt whiskies their characteristic tang.
(Matthew Gloag & Son Limited)

a dressing machine. These can still be seen at many distilleries and at flour mills where they are used for cleaning the grain for use. Although, traditionally, whisky was made only with locally grown barley, increasingly from the late eighteenth century barley was imported from England, Ireland and Europe, particularly the Baltic.

Today very little malt is made using traditional floor maltings and drying kilns. In the early 1960s Saladin box maltings were installed at some distilleries as there was insufficient labour to carry out the traditional process and demand was escalating. In this process the barley is loaded into a long concrete trough with a perforated floor. Air passes through the sprouting grain, which is continuously turned automatically by archimedian screws. Tamdhu distilleries on Speyside has large maltings of this type serving the distilleries of its owners, Highland Distilleries plc. Saladin plant was soon superseded by huge drum maltings, capable of producing large quantities of malt in an almost continuous process. It was the advent of this process in the 1970s that led to the closure of most of the maltings at distilleries and of many independent malting businesses throughout Britain. The malt arrives by lorry at most distilleries and sometimes by ship, when it is stored in large hoppers to rest for a few weeks.

The first stage of whisky making is almost the same as that of beer. For this reason distilleries often become breweries and breweries distilleries, as in the case of Oban distillery in Argyllshire. The malt is ground into a coarse flour or grit, not dissimilar to the consistency of oatmeal. Originally this was done using millstones driven by water power. If there was no mill at the distillery, the malt would have been ground at the local mill. Because of the need to grind the malt, distilleries were often situated adjacent to mills. The Gaelic for mill is 'vulin' and throughout the Highlands there are many places whose name ends in this way. There are two malt distilleries which bear this name, Lagavulin on Islay and Tamnavulin on Speyside.

Water is a vital and mysterious ingredient in the making of whisky.
(British Gas Scotland)

The miller was an important member of rural society, providing an essential service not only to the distillers and brewers but to the whole local community. From the middle of the nineteenth century stone grinding of flour began to give way to roller milling. By the end of the 1880s roller milling had been widely adopted. Distilleries installed simple compact belt-driven malt mills that crushed the grain between pairs of steel rollers. These are still universally used today. The rollers have to be set carefully to ensure that the grist contains the correct mixture of husks, pieces of kernel and dust. The quality of the grist is checked regularly. The grist passes normally by gravity feed to a hopper in the mash house.

As well as barley the other essential ingredient in the manufacture of whisky, perhaps more so than beer, is water. It is water more than anything else which gives each whisky its distinctive quality. Soft peaty water, like that commonly used in Islay and in the once large Campbeltown whisky trade, makes for heavier whiskies, while the harder waters of Speyside make for lighter styles. Distilleries draw their water from a variety of sources: some depend on deep wells and springs and others on streams and rivulets. Whatever its source, the water supply is jealously guarded and protected in the title deeds of the distillery. In places where two distilleries shared the same source of water, there were in the past legal wrangles about rights. In some places water can be seen flowing into the distillery along attractive stone-built lades. Apart from the water used in making the whisky itself, distilleries require great quantities of water to condense the distillate and, until recently, to drive the water-wheels and power the steam-engines. Water-wheels have been preserved at a few distilleries as an attraction.

The whisky making process begins in the mash-room. Here the water is heated to a temperature of between 60°C and 68°C, when it is termed liquor. The grist and liquor are then run together into a mashing-machine, a large copper tube with a rotating screw. The resulting porridge or mash is discharged into a large vessel known as a mash-tun, made usually from cast iron panels. The mash is stirred continuously by revolving rakes to allow the natural enzymes – diastase – in the malt to release the remaining starches into the liquor and convert them into sugars. The sweet liquid called 'wort' is then run off through perforated plates in the floor of the mash-tun into the 'underback'. As the husks and grains left in the mash-tun still contain some sugars, the residual porridge is treated with water at a higher temperature. This water is kept back to be used as the first liquor at the next mashing. The spent grains or draff in the mash-tun have always been used as animal feed, an important element in the agricultural economy of remoter Highland areas. Some distilleries have replaced their traditional mash-tuns with stainless steel 'lauter' tuns introduced from the German lager industry and which give better rates of extraction.

The wort held in the 'underback' is pumped through a refrigerator or a cooler to bring the temperature down to between 22°C and 24°C. It is then pumped to the tun-room and discharged into fermenting vessels called 'washbacks'. Every distillery has a battery of usually six or more washbacks, traditionally made of larch but now more commonly made of stainless steel. They are large vessels 4.57 to 3.65 m deep. As the brewer needs to have access to the top of the washbacks, they are set in the floor of the tun-room. Yeast is added to the wort to start the fermentation process of converting the sugars into ethanol (alcohol) and small quantities of other compounds known as 'congeners'. During fermentation the wash froths violently producing quantities of carbon dioxide. It is an old trick of brewers to lift the lid of a washback and to invite the unwary visitor to have a smell. The lack of oxygen can overcome those who fill their lungs too enthusiastically. Sometimes the wash can bubble over and small boys used to be employed to beat it down with heather switches. This process was mechanised from the late eighteenth century. Today most washbacks are fitted with electric switches. These are rarely used as fermentation is much less violent than it used to be, as yeasts are more stable and the process more scientifically controlled. After about two days the fermentation dies down. By now the wort has become a malt ale called 'wash' containing between five and ten per cent of alcohol by volume. The wash is then pumped into the wash charger in the still-room. After the washbacks have been emptied they have to be scrupulously cleaned to prevent any danger of bacterial infection in the subsequent fermentation. The wooden washbacks are steam hosed and scrubbed down. The stainless steel vessels are easier to clean.

The distillation takes place in two copper stills, one larger than the other. These are pear-shaped with swan necks. Every distillery has stills of differing shapes and sizes, which contribute to the distinctive

The securely fastened spirit safe was introduced in the 1820s to prevent distillers from defrauding the Excise.
(Chivas Brothers Limited)

The gleam of burnished copper in the stillhouse. Every malt distillery has its own distinctive shaped still.
(Matthew Gloag & Son Limited)

flavour of every single malt. Some stills are wide and squat, others tall and thin. When stills are replaced or new ones added, the shape of the original stills are faithfully copied. The wash is pumped into the larger of the two stills, the 'wash still', where it is gradually brought to the boil. When the wash comes to the boil it starts to froth as it contains yeast. There is an ever-present risk that the still may boil over and ruin the whisky. When stills were heated by coal or peat, the still-man had to control the fire very carefully to prevent this happening. He was helped by ball indicators connected by chains to floats inside the still which showed how far up the still the boiling wash had risen. There was also the danger that the particles of malt and yeast might catch on the bottom of the still and burn, again spoiling the whisky. This problem was overcome from the late eighteenth century by fitting rummagers made of chain mail which, driven mechanically, scoured the bottom of the still during distillation. These twin hazards were greatly reduced with the introduction in recent times of steam heating. The steam is pumped through hollow cylindrical pipes inside the still called 'kettles'. Today stills are heated by steam, gas or coke. The temperature in the still can be accurately controlled using electronic sensors and micro-processors. Despite the intrusion of new technology, the still-room of a Scotch malt distillery is a most exciting place, warmed by the heat from the burnished copper of the stills and redolent with the delicious aroma of whisky.

As the wash boils the vapours that are given off rise up the neck of the still and are passed over the neck of the still where they are condensed. The distillate from the wash is known as low wines. Traditionally condensation took place outside the still-house in a spiral copper tube, known as a 'worm', immersed in cold flowing water contained in a large wooden vessel called a tub. There are now very few distilleries that still use worms. Since the Second World War they have been replaced by shell condensers which are more economical in the use of water than the worm and allow for more intensive operation. After the low wines have been condensed they pass through the spirit safe.

The spirit safe was developed in the mid 1820s as part of reforms to reduce fraud at distilleries. It consists of a long brass box, usually highly polished, with a glass door at the front secured by a stout brass bar with padlocks at either end. Until recently the key to one padlock was held by the manager and the other by the Exciseman resident at each distillery. Inside the spirit safe are two brandy-shaped glasses with a chute down which the distillate flows. This can be directed by a lever on the outside of the spirit safe to allow the still-man either to discard or retain the distillate without coming into contact with it. There are also hydrometers in the spirit safe, once again operated from outside, so that the specific gravity of the distillate can be tested. When the low wines have finished running and only water is being distilled, the process is stopped. Until towards the end of the nineteenth century, the liquid left in the still, known as 'pot ale', was simply run off into nearby streams, rivers or the sea. With the rapid growth of whisky making at that time, the large quantities of pot ale being discharged began to present a serious pollution problem. The distillers responded by finding various uses for pot ale as a fertiliser and a cattle fodder. Since the 1960s plants have been established to treat the pot ale and mix it with dried draff to produce animal fodder known as 'dark grains'.

The low wines are pumped into a receiver or charger above the smaller spirit still. They are then run into the spirit still where the second distillation that finally produces the whisky takes place. The process is exactly the same as in the low wines still, but this time the still-man must be careful to preserve only the centre cut of the distillate. The first vapours to be run off are called foreshots and contain higher alcohols that are unpleasant to drink. They turn cloudy when mixed with water – a test that the still-man can carry out in the spirit safe. The foreshots are directed back into the low wines receiver to be mixed with the next distillation from the wash still. When all the foreshots have been distilled, whisky starts to be produced. Known as 'new make', this is piped away to the spirit receiver. It is colourless and contains about 60 per cent alcohol by volume. Until the First World War when legislation was introduced prohibiting the sale of whisky matured in the wood for less than three years, new make was a popular drink. It was stocked by many public houses, particularly in industrial districts, and drunk as a chaser with beer. Pot still malt new make has a tang of iodine, but a distinctive whisky flavour.

Towards the end of the final distillation various oily compounds begin to vaporise that if retained would damage the flavour of the whisky. These are known as feints, also turning cloudy when mixed with water. Like the foreshots they are discarded by being returned to the low wines receiver. At the end of the process some residual low wines are left in the still. Known as spent lees they are run to waste. When the distillation in either the wash or low wines still has been completed, the stills are emptied and the whole process begins again. Each still is fitted with a trap door which allows a man to get inside to clean and repair it. Although all the whisky made in pot stills in Scotland is now malt whisky, this was not always the case. Before the First World War, pot still grain whisky was produced in large quantities in Scotland. This was made from a mash consisting of unmalted barley and other grains and about five per cent malt – necessary to produce the diastase that converts the starches in the other grain into sugars. This pot still grain whisky was mostly sold straight from the still under the generic name Irish Whiskey, as it was and is the process most commonly used by pot distillers in Ireland.

The new make whisky held in the spirit receiver in the still-room is then pumped into another receiver in the filling store. Here the spirit is filled into oak casks of differing size and name – quarters, American

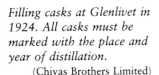

Filling casks at Glenlivet in 1924. All casks must be marked with the place and year of distillation.
(Chivas Brothers Limited)

barrels, hogsheads, puncheons and butts. Traditionally the finest malt whisky was filled into sherry casks, but these are increasingly difficult to obtain. Only Macallan distillery at Craigellachie now fills all its whiskies to be sold as singles into sherry wood. Other distilleries use a mixture of sherry wood and casks from America that have previously been used to mature bourbon whisky. Before use the inside of the casks are charred over an open fire. Originally all the larger distilleries had their own cooperages where barrels were repaired and rebuilt. Today most whisky companies have central cooperages or use specialist firms to meet their needs. Only simple repairs can be carried out at the distillery. The casks are filled through a bung-hole in the side of the cask. The bung, covered by a square of hessian, is then driven home. The ends of the barrels, which are colour-coded to show how many maturations they have been used for, are then stencilled with the name of the distillery, the date of distillation and a unique number to identify it. They are then ready to begin the long process of maturation in a cool dark warehouse, either at the distillery or elsewhere in Scotland. Not all the new make whisky belongs to the company which owns the distillery. Much of it is sold to other whisky or wine and spirit companies. The distillery maintains a register to show the owner of each barrel of new make and subsequent changes in ownership while it is in its custody. An annual rent is charged. Not all new make whisky is filled at the distillery where it is produced, but is taken away in tankers by customers to be filled on their own premises. To qualify as Scotch, the whisky must be distilled and matured in Scotland.

Traditional warehouses were cool, low roofed buildings where the barrels were stacked three high, separated by wooden stretchers, known as skids. Modern warehouses are tall cathedral-like buildings with barrels stacked as much as 20 high. Whatever the appearance of the warehouse, the process of maturation is the same. Since 1915 Scotch whisky has had to be matured for at least three years. Most malt whiskies are matured for much longer, usually for eight years, but not usually for more than 15 years. Each malt reaches perfection at a different age and some will peak twice in their life – early and late with a dull middle age. As it matures the whisky changes in character drawing colour and flavour from the wood. Some of the higher alcohols gradually change into esters and other compounds with delicate subtle aromas, strengthening the individuality of each whisky. About 15 per cent of the whisky in each cask evaporates during eight years of maturation – the Angel's share!

When mature the malt whisky is then ready for bottling. Unlike wine, whisky does not improve or deteriorate in the bottle. A small but increasing proportion of malt whisky is bottled as 'single' or 'self' whiskies for discriminating customers. In recent years it has become popular as an evening drink, taken with or without water and savoured slowly by the discerning who enjoy the intricacies of its complex flavour. It is hard to generalise about 'single' malts. They are all different and every one has its devoted admirers. On the whole the Islay and Campbeltown malts are heavier and more peaty than those from other islands and the Highlands, including Speyside, which are more delicate on the palate. Malts from the Lowlands are much blander, but nonetheless pleasant to drink. The final character and appearance of any single malt is influenced by the type of wood it has been stored in and the previous use of the barrels. Fino sherry wood will make for a lighter style, while oloroso wood will give a deep heavy rich whisky. The Scotch Whisky Society based in Edinburgh offers members the choice of malt whiskies matured in different types of sherry wood, which allows the connoisseur to appreciate variations produced at the same distillery. Any committed drinker of single malts should experiment, choosing from the now large range carried by the bigger wine and spirit merchants. Most malt whisky, however, finds its way into blends which account for the bulk of sales of whisky throughout the world.

In blended whisky malts from different distilleries are mixed in set proportions with grain whiskies distilled in patent or continuous stills. These stills were developed in the 1820s to overcome the need to empty and clean the pot still after each distillation. Although the first continuous still was perfected in Scotland in 1827 (see page 98), Aneas Coffey, formerly Inspector General of Excise in Ireland, designed in 1830 the patent still that became the standard method of making grain whisky. The Coffey still, as it is known, consists of two

Rolling a cask along skids in the warehouse at Highland Park Distillery in Orkney. This is a traditional warehouse with the casks stacked three high.
(Matthew Gloag & Son Limited)

The blending room at Robertson & Baxter's offices in Glasgow. The wall cabinets hold samples from malt and grain distilleries which provide the blender with the palette to make up the blends.

(Lang Brothers Limited)

copper columns, the analyser and the rectifier, which are divided into chambers by a series of perforated plates. The wash is brought almost to the boil by being pumped through the rectifier and is pumped into the top of the analyser where it meets low pressure steam injected at the bottom. As the wash falls through the analyser it vaporises and passes with the steam up the column and down to the base of the rectifier. The vapours ascend to the top of the column where they are condensed by the cold wash as it enters the rectifier. The water condenses at a lower level and falls to the bottom of the rectifier. Similarly, the spent wash descends to the base of the analyser and is pumped away. Although the Coffey still has been improved in recent years, the basic design remains the same. The grain whisky produced in a Coffey still is between 94 and 96 per cent alcohol by volume. Like malt, the 'new make' is colourless but also has a characteristically whisky aroma. Not surprisingly it is far blander than new make malt and remarkably palatable. It is matured for at least three years in exactly the same way as malt. Patent whisky, when mature, is light brown in colour with a pleasant nose and a soft flavour. Only one single grain whisky is sold as such – 'Old Cameronbridge' – from the distillery of that name at Windygates in Fife. As this distillery has recently closed it will soon be withdrawn from the market.

The bulk of most blends is made up of grain whisky drawn from different distilleries. The grain provides the perfect foil for the richer texture of the malts. The number of malts in a blend and their proportion to grain whisky varies markedly. A blend that has a large amount of grain can be as good as one with many malts. The quality of each blend depends entirely on the skill of the blender who normally works far removed from the distilleries at the main office of

A mixed consignment of peat coals and barrels arrives at Glenlivet distillery by steam lorries and traction engines.
(Chivas Brothers Limited)

a whisky company. He receives and stores samples of new make and mature whisky, not only from distilleries that his company owns, but from those of competitors as he will inevitably need these to build his blend. The samples are nosed in tulip-shaped glasses by the blender to assess their quality and nowadays also examined scientifically. It is the blender's job principally to maintain the consistency of existing blends and occasionally to design new ones. He arranges for the whiskies to be assembled according to secret recipes in the blending hall. Here the barrels of malt and grain whisky to be used in the blend are disgorged into a trough in the floor. They are then pumped through filters into large vats where the blend is roused either by stirring or blowing air through it. Some blenders prefer to mix or vat their malts separately and then combine them in the correct proportions to produce the final blend. Not all that long ago, when there were many independent wine and spirit merchants and breweries in England and Wales all making and bottling blended whisky and other spirits, whisky merchants in Scotland did a big trade in selling malt mixtures for blending. When the whiskies have been judged to be thoroughly combined, the blend is either bottled or in some cases returned to casks for a few months, to marry.

Until the development of mechanical bottling machines in the late nineteenth century, all bottling was done by hand, using a 'boot and flogger'. Since bottles were in short supply, empty wine bottles were often used. Most customers, however, preferred to buy their whisky in cask or, more commonly, in earthenware 'piggies' – cylindrical containers covered in wickerwork to protect them in transit and with a handle at the top. These can be found regularly in antique shops and seen in displays in public houses and whisky visitors' centres. The name of the whisky merchant and the town is usually stamped just below the neck. Today all whisky is bottled on long mechanical bottling lines. Before bottling the whisky is reduced in strength to between 40 and 45 per cent of alcohol by volume. In a captivating process accompanied by the rattle and chink of glass, the bottles, advancing relentlessly along the lines, are filled, capped, labelled and boxed in cardboard cartons. The Scotch whisky is now ready to be sold throughout the world.

There are a great many blends on the market. Even more so than malts, there are enthusiastic supporters of different blends of Scotch in almost every country of the world. Preference for one blend in one place is due almost certainly to historical accident. In the late nineteenth century when there were far more whisky houses than there are today, pioneering agents developed local markets and their efforts are still reflected in today's sales. Despite the advent of intercontinental air traffic and attendant duty-free shops, there are only a handful of blends than can claim worldwide appeal. This is largely because selling and promotion in the different countries of the world are mostly in the hands of local agents who choose to support blends that have always been popular in their market. Because of the international appeal of Scotch and its reputation for quality, there is an ever-present danger of counterfeiting. The Scotch Whisky Association is constantly vigilant in seeking out false claims and bringing those responsible to court. The Association also acts to try and prevent unfair discrimination against Scotch through the imposition of high import tariffs, usually designed to protect an inferior local product.

Casks of Dalmore whisky are tested for quality and consistency by a master blender.

(Whyte & Mackay Distillers Limited)

Water of Life to 1823

Legend claims that St Patrick brought the precious secret of whisky making with him from Germany to Kintyre in the fifth century. Although the art of distilling was certainly understood as early as this, it is thought that alcohol was not produced in this way for another six hundred years because methods of condensing the liquor were not well enough developed. The first people known definitely to have distilled fermented liquor are the Arabs and it is believed that the craft was brought to northern Europe by men returning from the Crusades who had witnessed the miraculous restorative powers

Filling the bottles with whisky after the long process of maturation and blending.

(British Gas Scotland)

88

of spirits on the human body. Hence, distilled spirits soon became known as *aquavitae* – the water of life. The term is still used in many European countries to describe a variety of distilled products.

The earliest known reference to Scottish whisky is contained in the Scottish Exchequer Rolls for 1494 where an entry records the sale of 'eight bolls of malt to Frair John Co wherewith to make *aquavitae*'. King James IV, who was killed so tragically at Flodden Field, enjoyed his whisky. When he visited Inverness in 1506 the treasurer of the burgh had to supply *aquavitae* for the King.

Scotch Whisky is the hallmark of quality. Modern quality control joins distillers and blenders in ensuring that every bottle matches its reputation.
(United Distillers)

At this time the distillate was condensed by the air and consequently production was limited. *Aquavitae* was used chiefly as a medicine. For this reason the Guild of Surgeon Barbers in Edinburgh was granted a monopoly over its manufacture in 1505. During the sixteenth century, however, the technique of passing the outlet pipe through cold water was introduced and the copper worm developed. At the same time the familiar pear-shaped still was introduced, preventing unpleasant flavours and noxious substances tainting the spirit. As a result the distilling of alcohol increased rapidly throughout those parts of Europe where it was too cold to grow vines.

By the 1570s whisky making was well established in Scotland. The introduction to an Act of the Scottish Parliament in 1579 complained that so much malt was being used in distilleries, grain for food was in short supply. The first excise duty on spirits was imposed by the Scots Parliament in 1644 to help finance the covenanting army in the rebellion against Charles I. It was reduced under Cromwell's direct rule and abolished at the Restoration of Charles II. By this time whisky drinking had become popular in every part of Scotland. At the 'wake' of Sir Donald Campbell of Ardnamurchan in 1651 the largest item on his funeral account was £84 Scots for five gallons (nine litres) of *aquavitae*. This whisky would have been distilled in one of the many small distilleries scattered throughout the country. In 1655 Robert Haig, an 'aqua brouster', whose family name is still well known to whisky drinkers, was accused of having 'his cauldron on the fyre, and a stand reiking' on the Sabbath day. Many distilleries were leased from the 'lairds' who received part of the rent in kind.

By the end of the seventeenth century there was a small number of larger distilleries, notably the Ferintosh distillery, near Dingwall in Ross and Cromarty, owned by Duncan Forbes of Culloden. He was a supporter of the Protestant King William III who, in 1688, ousted the Roman Catholic King James II. Duncan Forbes' estates were ransacked the following year by the Jacobites fighting for James. In recompense the Scots Parliament granted the Forbes family the right to distil whisky free of duty forever. This privilege was maintained after the Union of the Scottish and English Parliaments in 1707. The disturbances in the Highlands over the next 60 years, culminating in the rebellion of 1745 led by Bonnie Prince Charlie, prevented the family from making the most of their privileges. It is reputed that Bonnie Prince Charlie drowned his sorrows in locally made whisky after his defeat nearby at Drummossie Muir in 1746 at the Battle of Culloden. In the 1750s John Forbes re-established the distillery and started selling whisky as far away as Glasgow and Edinburgh.

By then the distilleries in the Lowlands had become more commercial, encouraged by the Gin Act of 1736 which imposed heavy duty on gin in an effort to stem drunkenness, but exempted *aquavitae*. During the next two decades commercial distilleries were set up in many towns. There was a setback in the 1750s when the Government prohibited distilling throughout the United Kingdom for three years as a result of a disastrous series of crop failures. The ban, however, did not extend to private stills which everyone in Scotland had the right to use to make whisky for their own use providing they did not sell it to anyone else. Not to be denied their whisky by the dictate of a government in London, privately distilled whisky began to be smuggled on a vast scale. During the 1760s it was reckoned that the private distillers were making ten times more whisky than the licensed distillers who had re-opened after the ban. The Excise authorities were powerless to do much to combat the smugglers. John Forbes, with his duty-free exemption, was able to withstand the competition, building three more distilleries on his estate and earning the then large sum of £18 000 profit a year.

Dram taking became a part of daily life, especially in the Highlands. In the novel *Humphrey Clinker* published in 1771, Tobias Smollett, himself from Loch Lomondside, noted:

When the Lowlanders want to drink a cheer upping cup, they go to the public house, called the Change House, and call for a champion of twopenny, which is a thin yeasty beverage, made of malt, not quite so strong as the table-beer of England . . .

The Highlanders, on the contrary, despise this liquor, and regale themselves with whisky, a malt spirit, as strong as geneva, which they swallow in great quantities, without any sign of inebriation: they are used to it from the cradle, and find it an excellent preservation against the winter cold, which must be extreme on these mountains – I am told that it is given with great success to infants, as a cordial in the confluent smallpox.[2]

The dram was a whole gill at about 60 per cent alcohol by volume, roughly equivalent to half a bottle of modern whisky. When Samuel Johnson made his famous journey to the Western Islands of Scotland in 1773, he and his companion, James Boswell, were regularly offered whisky to accompany their meals. At Coriatachan in Skye he noted that the typical Hebridean

as soon as he appears in the morning, swallows a glass of whisky; yet they are not a drunken race, at least I never was present at much intemperance; but no man is so abstemious as to refuse the morning dram, which they call a skalk.[3]

At Inveraray he took a dram, himself, as an experiment, finding it 'preferable to any English malt brandy . . . What was the process I had no opportunity of inquiring, nor do I wish to improve the art of making poison pleasant'.

Legal distilling started to recover in the late 1770s, almost certainly because the licensed or 'entered' distillers agreed to band together to defeat the smugglers by flooding the market with cheap whisky. They were helped by the lairds and farmers who were worried by the activities of the smugglers and the growth in imports of French

The workforce and excise officials at the Glenlivet distillery in the 1890s. The maltmen are in the front row with their wooden shiels.

(Chivas Brothers Limited)

wines and brandies. Throughout Scotland meetings of farmers in 1777 pledged not 'to use in their own houses any foreign spirits' but instead to drink 'malt liquors of the manufacture and produce of our own country'. The Government banned private distillation in 1781 and authorised the Excise to seize stills and spirits, calling on the military to help if necessary. A premium of one shilling and sixpence (7p) was offered to anyone who reported an illegal still. The wily Highlanders handed in their old broken stills and used the premiums to buy new ones! The Excise authorities' power was increased in 1783 when they were allowed to take possession of horses, vehicles and boats used for carrying contraband whisky. As a result there were many fierce battles between Excisemen and smugglers, with the smugglers often coming off best. Every district in Scotland has its own stories about such confrontations. Although what was now 'illicit' rather than private distilling and smuggling continued, the licensed distillers were able to enlarge their business in the Lowlands. Here the trade came to be dominated by two closely related families – the Steins and the Haigs.

By the close of the 1770s, James Stein's Kilbagie distillery in Clackmannanshire was the largest in Scotland, exporting spirits in great quantities to England to be converted or 'rectified' into gin. He loaned money to his relatives to establish large distilleries in Edinburgh and at Kincaple near St Andrews to serve both the Scottish and English markets. They were soon distilling on a massive scale using grain imported from Europe. By 1784 they were making over 400 000 gallons (1.82 million litres) of whisky a year for export south of the border. With foodstuffs in very short supply in Scotland in the early 1780s due to further poor harvests, the Haig and Stein distilleries were attacked by mobs and fiercely criticised. The Lowland farmers reminded their tenants that 'these distilleries saved imports and contributed directly to agricultural prosperity'.

Licensed distilling in the Lowlands was given additional impetus in 1784 with the passing of the Wash Act which simplified the regulations under which whisky was made and reduced duty. At the same time the Forbes family's right to distil duty free whisky at Ferintosh was withdrawn, prompting Rabbie Burns, who adored his dram, to pen his much-quoted poem 'Thee Ferintosh! O Sadly Lost'. The Wash Act also set out to stimulate the legal trade in the Highland counties by providing for lower rates of duty for whisky made in small stills out of barley grown in the parish. The lairds were unhappy with this provision as they were to be held responsible if the law was broken and the Lowland distillers feared that it would give rise to unfair competition. Consequently, the following year the legislation was amended, preventing the new Highland distilleries from exporting into the Lowlands and absolving the lairds of any responsibility for infringement. Immediately many lairds fostered the establishment of distilleries on their estates.

Sir Edwin Landseer's romanticised view of an illicit distillery. The detail of production is remarkably accurate. The lady has a small barrel or anker under her arm.

(United Distillers)

In the Lowlands the effect of the Wash Act was dramatic. Existing distilleries were enlarged and new distilleries opened. Legal output for Scottish consumption almost doubled to over 800 000 gallons (3.64 million litres). Production for exports to England reached nearly 900 000 gallons (4.09 million litres) by 1786 to the annoyance of the great London distillers who had, until then, enjoyed a monopoly of the market in the metropolis. A price war soon developed described by the banker, Sir William Forbes, 'as a foolish and fruitless contest with the London distillers, who, being an opulent body of men, had kept down the price of spirits in order to drive their Scotch competitors out of the market'. By December 1785 many of the larger distilleries in Scotland were facing ruin due principally to over-production. The law was altered again in 1786 and, as a result of intense lobbying by the London distillers, duty on export of spirits from Scotland to England was pitched so high as to amount almost 'to a prohibition'. The Stein and Haig families did all they could to hold on to their trade, including both suing and bribing the Excise.

James Burnet, the last Captain of the Edinburgh Town Guard, in the 1780s.
(Scotch Whisky Heritage Centre)

They failed. Their position was made impossible in February 1788 by yet another Act which required them to give a year's notice of an intention to export to England. Effectively prevented from exporting to England for a year, the five largest distilleries, producing 50 per cent of all the whisky made in Scotland, ceased trading at the end of the month with debts of over £700 000 – a colossal sum for the period. Unable to export the stock to England, the creditors had no alternative but to flood the Scottish market, causing problems for other licensed distillers and leading to more bankruptcies.

Despite the scale of their disaster, the Stein and Haig families were quickly back in the business, re-opening one of their Edinburgh distilleries in 1790. The difficulties of the Lowland distillers were magnified three years later when duty was tripled to help pay for the war with Revolutionary France. As duty was assessed at a flat rate on the capacity of the stills, the larger distillers sought to avoid paying at these punitive rates by devising means of producing whisky very rapidly in shallow stills to achieve the maximum throughput. The resulting whisky was harsh and not altogether palatable, but remained cheap. Distilling was banned altogether in between 1795 and 1796 due to shortages of grain, and duty increased. Some Lowland distilleries simply remained closed, those that re-opened began working their stills faster than ever with almost military precision. The trade in the Lowlands was dominated as before by a handful of large concerns, including those owned by the Steins and the Haigs, John Harvey at the Yoker distillery outside Glasgow and George Milne at St Clements Wells distillery at Tranent, East Lothian.

The Highland distilleries were protected by the 1785 legislation from the worst effects of the crisis in the Lowlands. Here small still whisky making flourished using traditional techniques and slow distillation to produce a fine flavoursome product. By 1798 there were 58 distilleries operating in Highland counties, producing between 1000 (4546) and 2000 gallons (9092 litres) a year. They were operated mostly as a part-time activity by local farmers and tradespeople who sold the bulk of their whisky in the immediate neighbourhood. As in the Lowlands, duty was tripled in 1793. The definition of the Highlands was also altered in 1795 to exclude Campbeltown, which had become the centre of distilling in the west of Scotland. These changes and punitive taxation combined to drive many licensed distilleries underground. Illicit distilling became widespread once again; fine Highland whisky was soon being smuggled in large quantities to the Lowland towns where it was considered to be superior to the harsh rapidly distilled whisky on the open market.

This unlawful trade was well organised with maltsters in towns like Campbeltown supplying malt to a network of illicit distillers operating very small stills. Many of these were worked by women, who faced less severe penalties if they were apprehended. When the whisky had been made, arrangements for it to be smuggled to the Lowlands or disposed of locally were made by the maltster. The Excise service was neither large enough nor endowed with sufficient legal powers to combat smuggling on such a scale. By the end of the century it was reckoned that a huge quantity of Highland whisky was pouring into the Lowlands, making it difficult for the licensed distillers there to remain in business, particularly after a further swingeing increase in duty imposed in 1797. Following howls of protest, the Government established an Inquiry to investigate whisky distilling in Scotland. Many of the recommendations to combat illicit distilling were not implemented because the Government was preoccupied with the more important task of fighting the war with France. However, the higher rates of duty were confirmed and measures taken to prevent avoidance by improving techniques of rapid distillation.

At the turn of the century there was a sequence of bad harvests, leading to another ban on distilling malt and other grains in 1801 and 1802. This was reimposed between 1809 and 1811 when crops again failed. During these years the larger distilleries owned by the Steins and the Haigs returned to exporting much of their spirit to England, making their washes from sugars when distilling from grain was prohibited. This relieved pressure on the Scottish market, allowing the other licensed Lowland distilleries to enjoy a degree of stability. The Excise service in the Highlands was strengthened following the Government Inquiry and efforts made to secure the support of the lairds in stamping out illicit distilling. Some acted harshly, evicting tenants who were caught, but the majority turned a blind eye.

Dram taking reached epidemic proportions. Elizabeth Grant of Rothiemurchus, who spent part of her childhood at the family home on Speyside, recalled that:

the whisky was a bad habit, there was certainly too much of it going. At every house it was offered, at every house it must be tasted or offence would be given so we were taught to believe. I am sure now that had we steadily refused compliance with so incorrect a custom it would have been far better for ourselves, and might all the sooner have put a stop to so pernicious a habit among the people. Whisky drinking was and is the bane of that county; from early morning till late at night it went on. Decent gentlewomen began the day with a dram. In our house the bottle of whisky, with its accompaniment of a silver salver full of small glasses, was placed on the side-table with cold meat every morning. In the pantry a bottle of whisky was the allowance per day, with bread and cheese in any required quantity for such messengers or visitors whose errands sent them in that direction.[4]

Concern was expressed in the early 1800s about the scale of intemperance by church leaders and others who deplored the encouragement given to illicit distillers by the lairds. Illicit whisky continued, however, to flow freely. The famous novelist, Sir Walter Scott, who loved a dram and cigar, boasted in 1813, 'I have plenty of right good and sound Highland Ferintosh'.

The following year after the defeat of Napoleon, the Government in London extended the rules under which English distillers worked to the whole of Scotland. These were wholly inappropriate, designed for making spirits for rectification into gin rather than the fine malt spirits produced in the Highland small stills, which were outlawed. Although the Scottish Board of Excise won concessions from the Treasury allowing the use of small stills to continue in the Highlands and permitting Highland whisky to be sold in the Lowlands, these were blocked in the courts by the large Lowland distillers. The effect of these measures, coupled with a serious economic depression after the War, crippled the whisky trade. Legal production slumped and illicit distilling flourished more than ever to the alarm of the Scottish Board of Excise which instituted an inquiry. There was strong pressure for the removal of the prohibition on exports to the Lowlands and for a cut in duty to make illicit distilling less attractive. In 1816 the Small Stills Act was passed permitting the use of stills of not less than 40 gallons (181 litres) using slightly weaker washes rather than the strong ones introduced two years before. The Highland line was abolished and duty throughout Scotland reduced. Immediately new licensed distilleries began to be opened throughout the country. There were just twelve licensed distilleries in the Highlands in 1816; by 1819 the numbers had risen to 57. It soon became apparent that the washes were too strong and the Highland distillers could not achieve the same quality as that produced by the illicit distillers. Consequently smuggling was hardly affected. The best illicit whisky was reputed to come from Kintyre and from the Glenlivet area of Speyside. The more skilful smugglers mixed small quantities of these flavoursome whiskies with other whiskies to produce a rudimentary blend. Clashes with the Excisemen became more violent as the smugglers sought to prevent any attempt to interrupt their contraband trade.

The attitude of the Highland lairds was, however, changing. In 1820 the Duke of Gordon, whose estates in the north-east included Glenlivet, pledged his support in the House of Lords for the eradication of illicit distilling, providing encouragement was given to the legal trade. Two years later the Illicit Distillation (Scotland) Act was passed imposing severe penalties for those detected distilling unlawfully or in possession of illicit whisky. Already, with the help of the landowners, the Excise had been bringing more and more cases before the courts. During 1822 alone more than 6000 cases were tried. The following year, under the Excise Act of 1823, positive encouragement was given to licensed whisky distilling. Duty

The magnificent view across to Glenlivet Distillery in Speyside.

(Chivas Brothers Limited)

was slashed and the weak washes that made smuggled whisky so palatable sanctioned. Export to England, where different rates of duty prevailed, was opened to all distillers without the need to register, breaking the stranglehold of the Stein and Haig families over the market to the south of the border. The Royal Seal of Approval was given to whisky in 1822 when King George IV made the first visit by a reigning monarch to Scotland for more than a century. Organised by Sir Walter Scott, the proceedings in Edinburgh were spectacular with the Highland chiefs in their full regalia. When the royal yacht arrived at Leith, Sir Walter Scott greeted the King who called for a bottle of Highland whisky to drink his health. This whisky was reputedly supplied by Elizabeth Grant of Rothiemurchus, who was instructed by her father to send to Edinburgh from the family's cellars 'whisky long in wood, long in uncorked bottles, mild as milk, and the true contraband goût in it' – the first recorded reference to maturation. After the King had drained his glass, Sir Walter asked to be able to keep it as a memento. He placed it in his coat-tail pocket carefully wrapped and returned home. When he arrived he found that the English poet, George Crabbe, had arrived unexpectedly. So pleased was he to see him that he sat down suddenly by his visitor and the glass was 'crushed to atoms'. His scream and gesture made his wife conclude that he had 'sat down on a pair of scissors or the like'.

Victorian Achievements: 1824–99

The success of the reforms in 1822 and 1823 was remarkable. The number of licensed distilleries at work in all parts of Scotland more than doubled in two years. Everywhere landowners encouraged the construction of new distilleries, often leasing them to trusted servants. Many of the new distillers depended for their know-how on the expertise of the illicit distillers who almost overnight had been driven out of business. Some of the new distilleries, like Oban distillery, were converted out of breweries. Campbeltown, with its well-established malting trade and reputation for illicit distilleries, emerged as the principal centre of whisky making. Over 37 distilleries opened in the town between 1823 and 1837. Although for some initial enthusiasm was quickly quenched by the harsh realities of the commercial world, a large number remained in being to lay the foundations of the modern trade. As Scotch whisky bore a lower rate of duty to spirits produced in England, an export trade to the north of England rapidly developed much to the annoyance of the brewers there.

In the mid-1820s Robert Stein, the owner of the large Kilbagie distillery in Fife, began to experiment with continuous distillation to avoid the costly and time-consuming cleaning of the pot stills each time they were worked off. By 1827 he had perfected a design which produced a very bland grain whisky cheaply and in large quantities. By 1831 there were three patent stills of this design working in Scotland and output soared, leading to the bankruptcy during that year of Andrew Stein who owned one of the new stills. While these developments were taking place in Scotland, Aneas Coffey, formerly Inspector General of Excise in Dublin, was addressing the same problem (see page 84). He had devised a more robust continuous still by 1830 which soon became known as the Coffey or 'patent still'. The first Coffey still to be installed in Scotland was at the Grange distillery at Alloa in 1834, which ceased trading within less than twelve months. After this initial setback further Coffey stills were installed with greater success. The advance in legal production in the late 1820s brought added concerns about over-consumption and drunkenness. Spirits were singled out as being far more injurious than beer or ale. From 1829 anti-spirits societies began to be formed throughout Scotland demanding the reduction of duty on beer and the increase of that on whisky. These demands matched by protests from English brewers about the favourable treatment of Scotch distillers were answered in 1830 when the Duke of Wellington's Government abolished the tax on beer, raised the duty on spirits in both England and Scotland, and removed the Scots distillers' right to recover duty paid in Scotland on spirits exported to England.

The Scotch whisky distillers were outraged by this threat to their livelihood and called for a reduction in the proposed levels of duty.

Steam lorries make their way to the Glenlivet distillery in the 1920s.
(Chivas Brothers Limited)

William Haig, owner of one of the largest distilleries in Scotland at Seggie near St Andrews, suspended operations on the grounds that he could no longer sell his produce south of the border. The 1830s and early 1840s were difficult times for the whisky makers with sales in Scotland flagging due to a decline in the economy caused in part by poor harvests. Many firms closed down. The number of working distilleries fell sharply from 230 in 1835 to 169 in 1844 and the number of Stein or Coffey stills in production fell from five to two. Revival came in the mid-1840s when several of the large Lowland distilleries began to re-equip with patent stills to serve the English markets, exporting their produce over the newly constructed railway network which now linked Scotland with Britain's major towns and cities. The repeal of the Navigation Acts in 1845, which freed trade to the colonies, opened up new potential markets where there were a large number of Scottish emigrants or Scottish soldiers. Within ten years grain whisky was being shipped in quantity to Canada, India, Australia, New Zealand and South Africa. Buoyed up by the growth in demand during the late 1840s and early 1850s, some of the Lowland distilleries became big businesses far larger in their scale of operations than the new mechanised breweries. In contrast the pot still malt distillers in the Highlands continued to operate on a small scale; but even they took advantage of the improved transport network to sell malt whisky further afield. The advance of patent distilling badly affected the malt producers. Sales dwindled and more firms were driven out of business. By 1856 the patent distillers were also in difficulties because too much whisky was being produced. The following year the six largest distilleries in Scotland agreed to divide their market for twelve months to avoid the danger of a price war.

Although the practice of blending whiskies had continued after 1824, there is no evidence that this was carried out according to set recipes. Better quality Highland malt whiskies, sometimes matured in sherry barrels, were randomly mixed with older malts and grain whisky, particularly for the public-house trade. The Highland malt distillers objected to this practice on the grounds that it debased their product. They changed their attitude during the 1850s when some of the bigger wine and spirit merchants, particularly those in Edinburgh, Glasgow, Perth and Dundee, began to adopt a much more scientific approach. Borrowing techniques from the French brandy industry they began vatting mature malts, that is mixing different whiskies from different distillations at the same distilleries to iron out variations. In 1853 Andrew Usher, who was the Edinburgh agent for the well-known Glenlivet distillery, made the first recorded blend of malt and grain whiskies to a set recipe – Usher's 'Old Vatted Glenlivet'. He began marketing this blend throughout the United Kingdom and overseas, particularly in India. Others quickly followed his example and the modern blend, lighter and more flavoursome than either a single malt or grain whisky, was born.

The equalisation of Excise duty in Scotland and England between 1853 and 1855 which pushed up prices and lowered demand south of the border persuaded more and more wine and spirit merchants to turn their hand to blending in the hope of securing sales elsewhere. Blending was further encouraged in the 1860s by legislation which allowed the blending and subsequent bottling to be carried out in warehouses away from the distilleries before duty was paid. Much of this early blend was not sold under proprietary brand labels like Usher's 'Old Vatted Glenlivet', but was bottled for grocers, breweries, wine merchants and others under their own labels. Blended whisky and some of the better vatted 'self' malted single malts began to appear in wine merchants' lists in all parts of the United Kingdom as an attractive alternative to brandy. Whisky production increased and malt distilleries were enlarged. At the end of the 1860s Cragganmore distillery was established on Speyside, the first new pot distillery to be opened for 20 years. The grain distillers, who already had too much capacity, sought to extend their agreements to share their market. These understandings reached fulfilment in 1877 in the formation of the Distillery Company Ltd (DCL), an amalgamation of six of the largest grain distilleries.

The following year the worst economic recession of the nineteenth century paralysed the whole wine and spirit trade, particularly in Glasgow where the City of Glasgow Bank failed in October. Luckily for whisky distillers the setback was only temporary due to the misfortunes of the French and Iberian wine and brandy producers, whose vineyards were devastated by the phylloxera beetle. Imported from America this pest, which attacked both the roots and foliage of vines, was first detected in the Rhone valley in 1863 and then spread rapidly. The output of cognacs fell by more than two-thirds in the 20 years from 1880 until the turn of the century. The records of Glasgow and Edinburgh wine and spirit merchants show that good quality brandy was almost unobtainable. Instead, as an excellent substitute, they turned increasingly to blended whiskies, registering their own brand names under the new Trade Mark legislation and investing in distilleries. For example, W.A. Robertson of the Glasgow wine and spirit merchants Robertson & Baxter decided to build a distillery at Bunnahabhain on Islay in 1880. Seven years later W.&A. Gilbey, a London wine and spirit merchant, bought the Glen Spey distillery at Rothes on Speyside. Blending and bottling halls were built in Scottish towns and cities equipped with huge vats for mixing the whiskies.

During the 1880s some wine and spirit merchants developed large markets for their brands, at home and abroad, particularly in the colonies. Haig & Haig won a considerable following in the United States for their brand 'Pinch' (sold as 'Dimple' in Britain). Wright, Greig, promoters of Dallas Dhu distillery (see page 117), exported their 'Roderick Dhu' blend in quantity to India and Australasia. By the end of the decade there was a bewildering number of blends, some with names drawn from Scottish history, some with topical titles and some simply called after the name of the proprietor. A few Highland malt distilleries sought to promote their whiskies as 'selfs', notably Glenlivet on Speyside and Talisker on Skye, which were always priced higher than all other malts. In 1887 a London journalist, Alfred Barnard, made a tour of all the distilleries in the United Kingdom which he published as a book. Illustrated with many line drawings, and written with enthusiasm for Scotland and Scotch, the book provided a fascinating insight into Victorian whisky making at this time.

There was a brief pause in the growth of the trade at the end of the 1880s but expansion was soon resumed. During the last decade of the century whisky enjoyed an unprecedented boom. New distilleries were constructed throughout Scotland, notably on Speyside which produced the increasingly popular lighter whiskies; John Dewar & Sons, whisky blenders in Perth, built Aberfeldy distillery between 1896 and 1898, and William Teacher & Sons established Ardmore distillery at Kennethmount in 1898. Many of the new distilleries were either built alongside railway lines or near the coast to expedite delivery and dispatch. During the 1890s the largest whisky merchants began to push their brands heavily at the expense of the grocery trade. Some like the Dewars in Perth and James Buchanan with his 'Black & White' and 'House of Commons' brands were remarkably successful. The bigger brands were advertised heavily competing on equal terms with mass-produced beer. The most spectacular promotions were staged by the firm of Pattisons of Leith which launched blends to suit every occasion, including one in doubtful taste to commemorate the death of General Gordon at Khartoum in 1885. The partners in the business speculated heavily in whisky stocks as the boom gathered momentum. In 1899 the firm collapsed with debts of over £½ million, foreshadowing a slump in the industry. As more and more blends incorporated mature whisky, stocks throughout the trade had reached a staggering 90 million gallons (409 million litres).

The Long Haul: 1900–59

Britain enjoyed a period of unparalleled prosperity at the end of the nineteenth century, which came to a sudden end in 1900. There followed ten difficult years, made worse for the whisky trade by a change in popular taste following the death of Queen Victoria in 1901. The new King Edward VII abhorred the heavy sweet wines enjoyed by his mother, preferring lighter drier wines, particularly champagne. Whisky sales fell back, hitting hardest the grocery trade and the market for self malts. Brands came to dominate the market and sales continued to increase despite the difficulties. DCL, which had been established to defend the grain whisky distillers, began to acquire Lowland distilleries to prevent cut-throat price cutting. In the Highlands small inefficient pot distilleries were driven out of business. Those pot distilleries, which had been most active in selling their whiskies as 'selfs', mounted a campaign to prevent patent still grain whisky and by implication blend from being termed whisky. Matters came to a head in 1905 when the Islington Borough Council decided to prosecute wine and spirits merchants for selling whisky 'not of the nature, substance and quality demanded'. The malt distillers emerged victorious. DCL responded by launching seven-year-old Cambus patent still whisky to demonstrate that grain whisky was Scotch. The Government appointed a Royal Commission in 1908 to adjudicate, which reported a year later that both patent still grain whisky and pot still malt whisky qualified as Scotch.

By the time the result was known Lloyd George, the Liberal Chancellor of the Exchequer and a confirmed teetotaller, had introduced his reforming People's Budget, increasing duty on whisky by a third. On hearing the news one Glasgow whisky merchant is reputed to have declared that his firm might as well stop trading. The immediate consequences were as Lloyd George had perhaps intended, dramatic: whisky consumption retreated and many firms of both distillers and whisky merchants found themselves in difficulties. The three largest blenders, John Walker & Sons Ltd of Kilmarnock, John Dewar & Sons, and James Buchanan & Co., investigated the possibility of amalgamation. The disruption of the trade was not as serious as at first had been feared due to a sharp recovery in the economy after 1911. Sales bounced back and blenders began to lay down stocks once more. The outbreak of War in August 1914 at first brought higher sales as more and more people found employment in munitions work. When by early 1915 the Allies had failed to score a decisive victory, Lloyd George, quite irrationally, blamed drink which he believed 'was doing more damage in the war than all the German submarines put together'. The Central Control Board (Liquor Traffic) was established with the remit of cutting consumption. To head off a draconian increase in duty in the budget the whisky distillers agreed only to sell whisky that had been matured in the wood for at least three years, because temperance organisations had always advocated that new made whisky was harmful. Meanwhile the Central Control Board took stiff action against the drink trade through a maze of rules and regulations. In the face of such a concerted attack on their livelihood and finding barley hard to obtain, blending houses and distilleries were put up for sale. DCL, led by its managing director, William Ross, worked hard to preserve the trade in the expectation that after the end of hostilities there would be a return to less punitive Government attitudes. DCL took over pot malt distilleries in the Highlands and the Lowlands and in 1916 began buying blending houses.

Conditions became more severe in 1916 when the Control Board cut production of pot still whisky to 70 per cent of the average of the five preceding years. With the acceleration of the German U-Boat campaign in the following year, pot distilling was banned altogether. The price of malt whisky soared. The patent stills were permitted to remain open because they made bakers' yeast as an important by-product. At the same time the Control Board determined to reduce the strength of whisky on sale to the public from about 60 per cent of alcohol by volume to less than 30 per cent. After a bitter wrangle, strengths were reduced to 42 per cent and finally to 40 per cent, which has remained the norm ever since. The whisky trade was also instructed to cut their sales to 50 per cent of those in 1916 in an effort to conserve the dwindling supplies. Prices of blend reached record levels. In May 1917 the Whisky Association

Washing bottles in W. & P. Lowrie's bottling hall in Washington Street, Glasgow, in the 1890s.
(Scotch Whisky Heritage Centre)

Bottling and packaging John Buchanan's House of Lords whisky in W. & P. Lowrie's bottling hall in Glasgow in the 1890s.
(John Hume)

was formed to speak for distillers and blenders alike in further confrontations with the Government. These occurred sooner than the new Association would have liked. Within a year all exports of Scotch had been prohibited and duty doubled to £1.10 shillings (£1.50) per gallon to raise revenue to help pay for the War. A system of fixed prices was introduced which prevented all the increase in duty being charged to the consumer. With the coming of peace in November 1918 whisky makers – like the whole country – looked forward to a period of prosperity. Early in 1919 the whisky available for home consumption was increased and the ban on pot distilling lifted; but duty was raised by two-thirds to prevent blenders from earning exorbitant profits out of their increased sales. Worse, the fixed prices were only increased to allow half the additional duty being passed on. By now virtually all Scotch whisky was bottled in blend because stocks of malt were too low to sustain the once significant trade in 'selfs'.

The initial reaction of some blenders to this attack was to sell out. During 1919 DCL took over John Haig & Co., the family business of Field Marshal Earl Haig the British Commander-in-Chief at the end of the War, and also Andrew Usher & Co. which could claim to have given birth to blending. Despite all the difficulties most distilleries had re-opened by 1920 and against the odds sales recovered to something like pre-war levels. During the winter the economy suddenly went into reverse, and remained in recession for much of the next 15 years. The outlook for whisky was made more gloomy by the prohibition in January 1920 of consumption of all alcohol in the United States, which had been one of the most significant export markets before the War. Sales of whisky declined steadily throughout the 1920s. At first output of malt and grain whisky held up to replace the stocks lost during the War. Shortages of mature whisky kept prices high persuading many families who owned whisky businesses to get out while the going was good. It was for this reason that the family shareholders in Robertson & Baxter, the Glasgow blenders, voted to sell their large stocks in 1922 to a consortium comprising John Buchanan & Co. and John Dewar & Sons, which had merged in 1915, and John Walker & Sons and DCL. An outcome of this deal was the revival of amalgamation talks which reached fruition early in 1925, when DCL took control of the three blending houses. Concerned that smaller firms might understandably feel threatened by this large grouping, William Ross went out of his way to reassure the whole trade that DCL's smallest customer would 'receive as in the past the same measure of justice as our most important buyers'. Two years later DCL also acquired White Horse Distillers, proprietors of the White Horse brand and two pot still malt distilleries. By then DCL controlled nearly all the major brands in the trade.

The malt distillers imprudently continued to build up stocks after the onset of the recession. In 1925 William Ross, warning of the consequences of over-production, launched a campaign to cut output by 25 per cent. The malt distillers required little convincing. Nearly 40 pot distilleries closed their doors in the next two years. However, by 1928 some decided that the reaction to falling demand had been overdone and production rose sharply. There was widespread price cutting, which made it difficult to earn any sort of return. During 1930 William Ross once again took the lead, closing some of DCL's distilleries and once more slashed production by a quarter. In the aftermath of the Wall Street crash and the crisis in the world economy few were willing to argue. Output plummeted by 40 per cent and both new make and mature whisky became difficult to sell. In 1933, with the exception of two distilleries, malt production was brought to a standstill in an effort to persuade the Chancellor of the Exchequer to reduce duty to stimulate home demand. This protest was of no avail. There was, however, a glimmer of hope on the horizon following the election of Franklin D. Roosevelt as President of the United States committed to the abolition of prohibition. Although blenders had found ways around the regulations by supplying whisky through off-shore agents and directly for medicinal purposes, there was a general belief that exports across the Atlantic would increase rapidly. This did not happen immediately as the United States authorities imposed a heavy import duty which was not removed until 1935. By then the world economy was struggling out of recession and British trade and industry were picking up. Whisky production recovered and prospects were better than they had been since the beginning of the century.

This improvement was short-lived. When war was declared in September 1939 duty was increased to help pay for the conflict. Early in 1940 output of both grain and malt whisky was pruned by one-third of the previous year's make by the recently established Government Committee on Brewing and Distilling. The Whisky Association took immediate action to conserve stocks by limiting its members' releases of whisky for sale on the home market to 80 per

A cooper's workshop at a distillery. Until recently all distilleries had their own coopers to mend casks.
(Chivas Brothers Limited)

cent of purchases in 1939. Further duty increases followed in April 1940 and at the same time the Government encouraged blenders and distillers to export as much as possible to the American market to help pay for badly needed war materials. Nearly seven million proof gallons (31.9 million litres) were shipped to the United States in 1940, more than two million gallons (nine million litres) more than in 1939. With barley and other grains in very short supply, the patent distilleries all ceased production in 1941 and pot distilleries either went on to short-time working or closed. By 1942 there were only 44 pot distilleries working, less than half the number in 1939. Output collapsed to under two million gallons, a little more than a fifth of the total quantity of malt whisky distilled in the last year of peace. The industry, nevertheless, continued to be urged to export as much as possible, shipping seven million proof gallons (31 million litres) in 1941, of which five million (22.7 million litres) was destined for the United States. Troubled by the fall in output and the large volume of exports, the Whisky Association cut releases to the home market to 50 per cent of sales in 1939. By this time, with the advent of the lend-lease scheme, there was no longer the same pressure to export to earn dollars.

In the spring of 1942 the Ministry of Food tried to force the Whisky Association to lift its restrictions on home sales. The Association refused to take such action unless more grain was made available for distilling. The Government replied by raising duty by a colossal 60 per cent. Later in the year, with the country's food supplies in jeopardy, supplies of grain for making whisky were cut off, and by the end of October 1942, all the distilleries in Scotland were closed. In the face of this crisis the Whisky Association changed its name to the Scotch Whisky Association to identify explicitly with the Scottish distilling industry. Although the Association tried hard to fix retail prices in the home market, a black market developed in whiskies distributed by bottlers and blenders who were not members. There was another large increase in duty in the 1943 budget to hold down demand even further. With the War beginning to turn in the Allies' favour, the Scotch Whisky Association and the Pot Still Malt Distillers Association were asked by the Ministry of Food to review peacetime prospects.

Both organisations were firmly of the opinion that the whisky trade would not be able to earn badly needed foreign exchange unless urgent action was taken to replace stocks. It was not until August 1944, with victory clearly in prospect, that the Ministry of Food made a limited supply of grain available for whisky making. Further supplies were released early in the New Year of 1945 on the understanding that a proportion of mature stocks would be reserved for export. Knowing that lend-lease would cease when the War was over, exports once more assumed a greater significance in Government thinking. Not long after VE day the Ministry of Food promised a large allocation of grains for the coming season. As had happened so often before the brighter outlook was quickly dulled. In July the general election returned a Labour Government, committed to improving living standards and tinged with anti-drink

The cooperage at W. P. Lowrie & Co. of Glasgow, showing a variety of barrels being rebuilt for the whisky trade.

(John Hume)

sentiment. By November it had become evident that the Ministry of Food had made wildly optimistic forecasts of the availability of cereals. Distillers were informed that it would not be possible to deliver the cereals that had been pledged by the outgoing wartime National Government. Early in 1946, the Minister, Sir Ben Smith, dismayed the whisky trade when he announced a policy of 'Food Before Whisky'. Production was limited to three-sevenths of the make in 1939, forcing most distilleries to close for the remainder of the season. With demand rising and stocks falling, most blending companies and distillers were reluctant to raise releases to exporters for fear that, within three years, they would be unable to satisfy the custom they had generated. With the Ministry unable to offer any cereals for the coming season, the Scotch Whisky Association unwillingly agreed to the Government's cutting back releases to the home market from January 1947 to 45 per cent of sales in 1939.

As many had predicted the sterling crisis of 1946 to 1947 forced the Labour Government to encourage exports to obtain hard currency overseas. Grain for distilling was only to be made available on the understanding that the blenders would concentrate on exports, particularly to the United States of America. After negotiations with the Scotch Whisky Association, the home market was rationed to 25 per cent of sales in 1939 from May 1947 and duty raised by over 20 per cent towards the end of the year. Prevented from selling at home the whisky trade turned its attention to overseas markets. Quotas were agreed between the Government and Scotch Whisky Association for each foreign country, with the emphasis placed on the United States. Although shipments in 1947 totalled 6.7 million gallons (30.5 million litres) with 3.9 million gallons (17.7 million litres) going to the United States, this was less than the Minister had expected. He told the Scotch Whisky Association that unless there was marked improvement, cereals would be diverted to cattle feed to save imports. The Association pledged the industry to releasing 10.5 million gallons (47.7 million litres) of mature whisky in the coming year. The Government raised duty and pruned releases to the home market to just 20 per cent of 1939 sales. Those in the wine and spirit trade today, whose memory stretches back to the immediate postwar years, can remember only too clearly the difficulties in obtaining whisky on the home market at the time. Often blenders could only supply a few bottles as a gesture. Despite the effort of both the Scotch Whisky Association and the Government, a black market flourished with whisky changing hands far in excess of the fixed price.

Exports by 1949 matched projections and more grain was released for distilling. The following year there was sufficient to meet the needs of both the grain and malt producers. The Labour Government suddenly abandoned control of home barley sales in 1949, leaving distillers free to buy in the open market. At first this made little difference as the harvest in 1951 was poor and barley prices high. From 1953 output recovered sharply. In August of that year the recently elected Conservative Government abolished the system of controlling releases to the home market and agreeing quotas for different overseas countries in return for an undertaking that the Scotch Whisky Association would administer a voluntary rationing scheme, giving greater flexibility, until stock could be expected to have been completely replenished in 1959. From 1955 distillers were free to import as much grain as they required. Output climbed swiftly. Distilleries were enlarged and new warehouses were constructed at almost every distillery. In 1957 Distillers Corporation – Seagrams Ltd of Montreal – constructed the first malt distillery, Glen Keith, to be built in Scotland since the end of the nineteenth century. Seagrams had entered the Scotch whisky trade ten years before, when they purchased Chivas Bros, a small blending house in Aberdeen. Demand for whisky throughout the world, but especially in North America, soared. The heroes and villains of feature films were regularly portrayed drinking whisky, contributing to its popularity. The price of mature whisky stocks for blending rocketed in 1958.

The beautiful Strathisla distillery at Keith.
(Chivas Brothers Limited)

1959 Onwards: Modern Success

Although with the ending of voluntary rationing in 1959, whisky could be sold freely anywhere, there was no incentive to disturb the pattern of exports built up over the previous decade. The United States continued to be by far and away the largest market with a bewildering number of brands on offer. Fifteen brands, however, dominated sales, of which four had some 50 per cent of sales – 'J & B Rare' owned by International Distillers and Vintners; 'Cutty Sark' owned by Berry Bros & Rudd, the London wine and spirit merchants and blended by Robertson & Baxter of Glasgow; and 'Dewar's' and 'Johnnie Walker' owned by Distillers Company Ltd. By the late 1960s the two DCL blends were overshadowed by 'J & B Rare' and 'Cutty Sark'. Other overseas markets were small by comparison throughout the 1960s. Except for DCL's 'Johnnie Walker', no brand could claim worldwide appeal.

The largest market outside North America remained the United Kingdom. Although the wartime National Government and its Labour and Conservative successors had maintained that the high levels of domestic duty were an expedient to stimulate exports, there were no reductions after 1959. In fact there were periodic increases during the following decade. DCL brands had traditionally had the largest slice of home sales, particularly 'Haig', 'Johnnie Walker', 'Black & White', and 'White Horse'. Competition intensified in the 1960s, with 'Teachers', owned by the Glasgow-based William Teacher & Sons, Seagrams 'Chivas Regal', and Arthur Bell & Son's 'Bells', all making inroads into DCL's sales. After the abolition of resale price maintenance in 1964, DCL hit back, cutting prices and offering across the board discounts. Their strategy, in direct contravention of William Ross's pledge in 1925, was to use the size and power of DCL to crush the competition. Production and distribution were streamlined to improve the service to the consumer. The whisky war reached fever pitch in the early summer of 1970 when DCL refused to follow the rest of the trade's lead in raising prices. However, the home market did not expand, principally due to the regular increases in the rate of duty.

The unprecedented export growth in sales of blended whiskies in the 1960s at around 10 per cent per annum, led the trade to forecast continued gains for at least another decade. Production, notably of grain whisky, was planned to generate stocks to sustain such expansion. Between 1959 and 1966 output of grain whisky more than doubled from just over 41 million gallons (186 million litres) to nearly 90 million gallons (409 million litres). New grain distilleries were built at Invergordon on the Cromarty Firth, Girvan in Ayrshire, and at Airdrie. There was an even greater advance in malt whisky production from 16 million gallons (72.7 million litres) between 1955 and 1956 to 51 million gallons (232 million litres) in 1966. Distilleries that had been closed since the interwar years were re-opened, like Glenturret near Crieff and Glenglassaugh near Portsoy, both rebuilt between 1959 and 1960, and Isle of Jura distillery and Caperdonich distillery, both reconstructed between 1963 and 1965. Four completely new malt distilleries were opened – Tomintoul, Tamnavulin, and Glenallachie, all on Speyside, and Loch Lomond distillery at Alexandria to the west of Glasgow. Many established distilleries were either enlarged or completely rebuilt.

In the less stable economic conditions of the early 1970s, combined with a sudden change in taste away from whisky towards white wine, exports of Scotch whisky failed to live up to expectations. The United States market was seriously affected with a sharp decline in sales in the opening year of the decade. During this period the leading six brands enlarged their markets, but smaller brands bottled in Scotland were squeezed by blends shipped in bulk and bottled in the United States. The stagnation of the market that had been chiefly responsible for the rapid expansion of the industry since the War forced whisky blenders to re-assess the potential of other areas of the world. In many countries customers and agents had been neglected in the headlong concentration of meeting the apparently insatiable demand from the United States. The DCL, which had maintained a semblance of representation worldwide, was able to switch quickly to other market areas, particularly central and southern America, Australia, Japan, Hong Kong, and the countries of the European Economic Community. Although sales of blends bottled in Scotland grew markedly in Japan, they were eclipsed by a massive increase in sales of bulk blend and malt which more than quadrupled from two million gallons (nine million litres) in 1971 to almost nine million gallons (33 million litres) by 1976. Much of this bulk export was used as ad-mixtures for whiskies locally produced using techniques learned in Scotland. Expansion outside the United States ensured that exports maintained their upwards trend, albeit at a slower rate, to the end of the decade. Even the home market began to advance in line with other spirits, encouraged by a small reduction in the rate of duty between 1973 and 1975. Following further sharp increases imposed by the Labour Government between 1975 and 1977, progress was curtailed.

In addressing the obvious latent demand in EEC countries after the United Kingdom gained membership in 1973, the whisky trade was hampered by the Commission's attitude to its long-established practice of appointing sole distributors/agents for different specified geographical areas. In return, the agent shouldered the burden of brand promotion and protection, and of financing stocks. The agent was left to determine the price structure to cover the cost of these services. When questions were raised about the legality of these arrangements under EEC rules, less scrupulous wholesalers in the United Kingdom, where price competition was severe due to the

Dalmore distillery founded by the Mackenzie Brothers in 1839 at Allness on the Moray Firth.

(Whyte & Mackay Distillers Limited)

activities of the DCL, began parallel exporting, particularly to Europe and, to a lesser extent, to Japan. This action threatened to undermine the position of the leading brands throughout the world, as it allowed them to appear on the shelves at a discount to those sold by the recognised agents with their substantial overheads. The industry went to the European Court seeking ratification of the long-established agency system. Since the whole concept of parallel trading is fundamental to the EEC, proceedings were inevitably slow. The DCL, which was most vulnerable, was unable to wait for the outcome and withdrew its leading export brand, 'Johnnie Walker Red Label' from the home market in 1977 and priced up its other labels. The effect was dramatic, with a sharp fall in market share, allowing independent blenders, like Whyte & MacKay and Highland Distilleries with its 'Famous Grouse' blend, to build their brands at home before setting their sights on export markets. It was not until 1983 that the Commission announced that a favourable decision would be made, but, even then, the industry had to wait a further two years for formal confirmation.

The changing pattern of overseas and domestic sales in the 1970s was accompanied by structural changes in the industry. The Glenlivet and Glen Grant Distilleries Ltd, Longmorn-Glenlivet Distilleries Ltd and the blenders, Hill Thomson & Co. Ltd, amalgamated in 1970 to form Glenlivet Distillers Ltd. Seven years later Seagrams acquired the company. Sir Hugh Fraser's Scottish & Universal Investment Trust bought Dalmore-Whyte & Mackay in 1972 and added Tomintoul Glenlivet Distillery Co. in 1973. DCL took over Mackinlays & Birnie, owners of Glen Albyn and Glen Mhor distilleries at Inverness in 1972 and in the same year Invergordon Distillers Ltd acquired two malt distilleries. Increasingly, whisky companies found themselves part of large integrated drinks groups. Watney Mann, the brewers, purchased International Distillers & Vintners in 1972, before being absorbed by Grand Metropolitan later in the year. In 1975 Allied Breweries bought William Teachers & Sons and Whitbread took over Long John International from the American concern, Schenley Industries Ltd.

Weakness in current demand, coupled with soaring interest rates, depressed production of both malt and grain whisky. Malt whisky output reached a peak in 1974 of 204 million litres of pure alcohol, falling to 169 million litres by 1977. Grain whisky output peaked a year earlier at 272 million litres of proof alcohol, dropping to 195 million litres in 1976. This decline worried many observers, who believed that, by the early 1980s, when an upturn was confidently predicted, there would be a serious shortage of stock. As a result, despite the financing problems, production was stepped up from 1977 for grain and from 1978 for malt. Total output for malt in 1978 exceeded the peak in 1974, and by 1979 grain production had come back almost to the level of the early 1970s. This recovery was short-lived. As the recession at the end of the decade began to bite, companies could not mobilise funds to lay down additional stocks even if they believed demand could be sustained into the late 1980s. Output of both malt and grain whisky retreated sharply, collapsing by 1983 to their lowest levels since the end of rationing in 1959. Many distillers were placed on part-time working and the number of people employed by the industry in Scotland fell from 25,000 in 1978 to just under 18,000 by 1984. Some distilleries closed permanently.

The recession in the world economy disguised underlying changes in consumer preference for alcoholic drinks, which was moving away worldwide from whisky towards blander style spirits and to wine. Overall, there was a decline in demand for all alcoholic beverages, partly through pressure on discretionary spending, but more significantly in the long term, in response to a revival in calls for temperance based on medical evidence of the consequence of immoderate drinking. The whisky trade took some time to recognise these factors, believing that the setback was due to economic rather than structural problems. This argument was given some credence by an upturn in sales in 1982 which encouraged distillers to predict growth of three per cent per annum for the rest of the decade. It was almost certainly on this assumption that the Conservative Government did nothing to help the industry in the domestic market, continuing to raise duty in line with inflation. The Government seemed content to continue the policy of holding up domestic prices to encourage exports, even though this was no longer either appropriate or necessary. Sales worldwide resumed their downward path in 1983 and the decline continued for the next two years. The industry lost confidence in predicting future sales patterns.

With clear signals that there was an underlying decline in demand worldwide, the industry re-assessed its sales strategy. The success of Highland Distilleries' premium priced 'Famous Grouse' in the home market had demonstrated that well thought-out and targeted

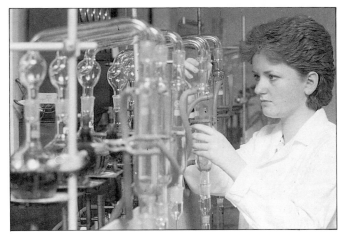

Above left: A modern bottling hall, alive with the clink and rattle of bottles moving along the filling lines.

(United Distillers)

Above right: United Distillers' research laboratory where the future quality of Scotch is assured.

(United Distillers)

promotion could win a market share as effectively as price competition. Others, including DCL, quickly followed suit, becoming more selective in discounting, concentrating their efforts on positioning their brands as far up the price range as prudent. This strategy inevitably led to the withdrawal of support for brands at the lower end of the market where returns were negligible. Although some commentators believed that the sole agency/distributor system was the only way of achieving effective worldwide sales coverage, there were growing doubts within the industry about the continuing viability of the system, particularly since many agents/distributors were being assumed into large international drinks conglomerates. The DCL was most exposed to such changes in ownership. During 1983, following the appointment of a new chairman, albeit from the ranks of the executive directors, there was a massive reorganisation of DCL management. Early in 1984 Somerset Importers, the distributors in the United States of 'Johnnie Walker Red Label' was acquired, heralding a policy of direct representation in larger export markets. The underlying strategy was to raise the value of sales rather than as had been the case in the 1960s and early 1970s, to shift bulk. By the end of 1985 there was plenty of evidence that DCL was not only earning higher returns, but also clawing back market share at a time when overall sales of Scotch whisky were falling. Throughout the second half of the year there had been regular press reports that the Argyll Group, whose principal business was food retailing in the United Kingdom, intended to bid for the company. Egged on by the press, the Argyll Group made a formal offer on 2 December for the company that still dominated the industry with 40 per cent of sales throughout the world.

DCL rejected the bid outright on the grounds that the two companies were totally incompatible. The management was disappointed that shareholders and the institutions equivocated in offering support. The Conservative Government, wedded to its free market philosophy, refused to refer the bid to the Monopolies Commission, even though in its first year of office in 1980 a much smaller bid by Hiram Walker for Highland Distilleries had been disallowed after referral. Uncertain of their chances in a straight contest, the DCL board chose early in 1986 to recommend a rival offer from Guinness plc, which had acquired Arthur Bell & Sons after a tough fight the previous year. The attraction for DCL in Guinness was its expanding team of marketing and sales executives deployed in 26 of the largest export markets. There followed one of the most bitterly contested and acrimonious take-over battles in recent times which seemed likely to set a new and unwelcome pattern in corporate behaviour. Guinness emerged victorious in April, but by the end of the year, serious questions had been raised about the legality of the bid. The Guinness board was reconstructed under a new chairman, Sir Norman McFarlane, responsible for welding the two companies into an integrated international drinks group. Despite the extensive press coverage, or perhaps because of it, whisky sales were not damaged by the Guinness affair. In fact, worldwide they increased during 1986 and remained buoyant into 1987. This upturn was characterised by sustained growth in premium priced blend and single malts, and a decline in export sales of bulk blend and malt, either for overseas bottling or as ad-mixtures to locally produced whisky

Today and Tomorrow

Despite the changes in ownership and in scale of production, Scotch whisky distillers and blenders are firmly committed to a traditional craft that dates back over five hundred years. For all the improvements in technology, the process of pot distillation remains the same. Although the patent still was not invented until the 1820s it developed naturally from long experience of distilling grain whisky in large pot stills. Blending, practised originally by the smugglers, offered an opportunity for the public to enjoy the best of both grain and malt. Its continuing popularity since Victorian times is testimony to the courage and foresight of those early pioneers whose names are still to be found on many a blend. During 1988 there was concern about the future of whisky, Scotland's most important foreign currency earner, aggravated by medical advice to cut personal consumption. Popular opinion in the United States moved strongly in favour of temperance, if not total abstinence. Scotch whisky makers, who had survived total prohibition in the United States during the inter-war years, were not to be deterred by the prevalence of such attitudes. Already there was general agreement that the attempts in the 1970s to make Scotch whisky a drink for all occasions at all times had been misplaced. The consequence had been over-production, a decline in quality and clear indications that for many drinkers familiarity was breeding contempt. The future lay in restoring Scotch whisky to its pinnacle as the finest of all whiskies that could hold its own with the very best of brandies. Such a commitment was not incompatible with calls for the temperate use of alcohol, but required distillers to avoid the temptation of always trying to match demand by raising output. Instead they chose the path, which French brandy makers had long pursued, of raising prices to impress on whisky drinkers the privilege of charging their glasses with such a valuable article.

This strategy to preserve the justified reputation of Scotland's national drink yielded rewards in 1989, with a growing confidence that the setbacks of the previous decade were now a thing of the past. A crucial element in this change in outlook was Guinness which, under its new management, was fast developing into a very professional integrated drinks company. DCL was renamed United Distillers with responsibility for the whole of the group's Scotch whisky interests. Building on the efforts made to overhaul DCL before the takeover, United Distillers totally reorganised their business, closing down many of the subsidiary blending companies, shutting some unwanted distilleries permanently, and unifying sales teams. Marketing became more professional, with a continuing

The Whisky Shop in Edinburgh shows the remarkable diversity of Scotch, with as many single malts as there are distilleries and countless numbers of blends.
(Della Matheson)

concentration on the leading clutch of blends, particularly 'Johnnie Walker' and six 'classic' malts drawn from Islay, the Highlands and the Lowlands. Visitor centres were developed at key distilleries following the example pioneered several years ago by Glenfarclas, Glenfiddich, and Glenlivet distilleries. The rest of the trade, long accustomed to competing with United Distilleries in its old guise as DCL, was not to be left behind by these developments. Packaging of all the leading blends became more attractive, with colourful boxes and cleverly designed presentational material. In a remarkably short time whisky's international image has been transformed. The potential for increased sales has been bolstered by the Japanese pledge to dismantle punitive trade restrictions designed to protect its own distilling industry. Exports of Scotch now total some £1.2 billion a year.

It would be a brave man who predicted an uncomplicated future for a trade whose history has been so bedevilled with vicissitude. Whisky, however, does now seem set fair on a course which will carry the quality of Scotland to every corner of the earth. For the visitor to the land of its birth, whisky makers have thrown open their distilleries, emphasising in their displays the close links between this generous spirit and the people of Scotland. In the heart of Edinburgh, not far from the Castle, is the Scotch Whisky Heritage Centre, opened in 1988 as a showcase for the trade (see page 119). There are still many blends on the market, 'Grants', 'Chivas Regal', 'Teachers', 'Mackinlays', 'Whyte & MacKay', 'Dewars', 'Bells', 'Long John', 'Famous Grouse', 'Cutty Sark', 'Ballantines' and 'J & B' to name but a few. They are all different and universally excellent. The same is true for the malts that can now be found in many wine merchants all the year round. The best advice for lovers of Scotch whisky is to be adventurous and savour the distinction of every dram.

Dallas Dhu Distillery

Dallas Dhu distillery, just south of the burgh of Forres in Moray in north-east Scotland, is now a Scottish Monument cared for by the Historic Buildings and Monuments Directorate in Scotland. Until 1986 the distillery was owned by the Distillers Company Ltd (DCL), which had closed it three years before. In an imaginative gesture, the company presented this handsome stone-built distillery to the Secretary of State for Scotland to allow visitors to see, as it were, behind the scenes of a typical malt distillery. With a minimum of alteration, but with a maximum of effort to create well-thought-out, meaningful displays, the distillery was opened to the public in 1988. The distillery was built between 1898 and 1899 at the height of the Victorian whisky boom by Wright & Greig, a Glasgow firm of whisky blenders. It was designed by C.C. Doig of Elgin, one of the best-known distillery architects of the time. He it was who introduced the pagoda roofs for the malt kilns that many people regard as an integral feature of distillery buildings. At the distillery the visitor can follow the process from the malting of the barley through mashing, fermentation, distillation and maturation. The malting floors and the kiln can be inspected. The tun-room has a life-size figure of the brewer testing the specific gravity of the wash to determine how the fermentation has progressed. In the still-room the figure of the still-man can be seen opening the valve to fill the wash still. The worms for condensing the distillate were never replaced at Dallas Dhu by heat exchangers and the visitor can see the large worm tubs outside the still-house with their intricate worms — testimony to the skill of Scottish coppersmiths. In the filling store a distillery worker is portrayed in the very act of filling a barrel with the bung beside him to drive home directly the job is done. In the distillery grounds are to be found the houses for the manager, the Exciseman and the workers. Alongside the site is the disused railway line to Aviemore — now a walkway — which was a critical factor in Wright & Greig's decision to locate a distillery here.

Wright & Greig was founded in the 1870s as wine, brandy and commission merchants. Like many other Scottish wine and spirit merchants the firm began to deal in whiskies towards the end of that decade when brandies and wines became scarce due to the ravages of the phylloxera in France (see page 100). Using their knowledge of blending gained in the brandy trade, it was a simple matter for such firms to begin blending whisky. Wright & Greig started selling their blend under the name 'Roderick Dhu' in the early 1880s. This name was taken from one of the characters in Sir Walter Scott's well-loved narrative poem *The Lady of the Lake*. The firm soon developed a flourishing export trade, particularly to India, Australia and New Zealand. The sudden collapse of the whisky boom at the turn of the century brought problems for Wright & Greig, forcing them to write-down their capital. In 1919 the company was liquidated and shortly afterwards Dallas Dhu was acquired by Benmore Distilleries Ltd, which took its name from a distillery in Campbeltown. In turn this firm was acquired by DCL in 1929 who closed Dallas Dhu temporarily the following year. The distillery, like many others, remained silent until 1936. Benmore distillery was dismantled, but the name was retained and can still be seen at the distillery. Dallas Dhu shared in the post-war whisky boom, but when whisky sales faltered in the early 1980s, it was closed permanently, largely because the water supply was inadequate.

The distillery is open all the year round and is well signposted on the road from Forres to Grantown-on-Spey. An attractive well-illustrated booklet describing the distillery and its history is available, published by the HMSO and available from their bookshops.

Scotch Whisky Heritage Centre

The Scotch Whisky Heritage Centre stands at the top of the Royal Mile in Edinburgh in the shadow of the Castle. It was established in 1988 to show the world how today's whisky makes its slow journey to the bottle and tells the story of the long history of whisky making in Scotland. As the visitor enters, the process of malting, mashing, fermentation and distillation are explained. There is malt to handle and a peat bank to touch. Visitors then literally walk through a washback, looking up to see the froth bubbling up on top of the fermenting liquor. There is a pause to watch an audio-visual display illustrating the diversity of whisky making and of the Scottish countryside. This is followed by a presentation of a magnificent model of a Highland malt distillery showing the process from the very beginning through to maturation. Then there is an opportunity to catch sight of a blending room and to nose whisky, appreciating the transformation of new make during its years of maturation and the differences between grain and malt whisky and the different styles of malt whisky. Next the visitor passes by a highly polished brass spirit-safe, through a faithful reconstruction of a warehouse, and upstairs to experience a flavour of the history of the trade.

The visitor journeys through the history, appropriately seated in a barrel. The story begins in the small farm distillery of George Orre, who made whisky at Ardchattan in Argyllshire in the seventeenth century. His home, which also provided shelter for his cattle and poultry, is typical of many Highland houses of the time. The visitor not only sees George Orre, but smells the reek of his pot and his animals, and hears the chatter of Gaelic voices. No sooner has the barrel moved on than the smell of fire and the crackling of burning timbers forewarns of the destruction of the Ferintosh distillery in 1689. This devastation gives way to prosperity with a glimpse of John Forbes counting the profits from his duty-free enterprise. No sooner has the chink of coin died on the ear than Rabbie Burns can be seen, glass in hand, bewailing the loss of his beloved Ferintosh in 1779. The architects of this tragedy stand smugly before the crowded wharfs of Leith docks where ships are waiting to carry their produce to London.

The barrel then carries the visitor on to a bleak windswept moorland, the haunt of an illicit distiller during the difficult times of the French Revolutionary wars. The distiller sits cloaked in his plaid, carefully tending his still while his helpmate and his dog keep a vigilant watch for the Excisemen. Unbeknown to them, an Exciseman is waiting, pistol in hand, to pounce. The smugglers then come into view carrying their contraband whisky in the dead of night into the very heart of Edinburgh under the nose of the town guard. Darkness is followed by brilliant light as the barrel travels

119

A family embarks on the Whisky Heritage Centre ride through the history of whisky with a representation of an early distillery at Ardchattan coming into view.

(Scotch Whisky Heritage Centre)

into George IV's visit to Edinburgh with Highland lairds standing in wait and Sir Walter Scott proffering a dram. Whisky making comes of age after 1823 with a recreation of one of the first new licensed stills in the Highlands and Aneas Coffey labouring over the designs of his patent still.

The barrel then takes the visitor through the dramatic development of the blender's craft with magnificent photographs of the interior of a nineteenth-century bottling hall. The success of Victorian blenders in winning an international market for whisky is portrayed in a dockside scene with a traveller leaving on a sales tour and crates of whisky awaiting despatch. The visitor learns of the problems of the whisky makers after the turn of the century and witnesses the evils of prohibition in America at the door of a speak-easy. The journey ends in festival mood, with the triumph of Scotch after the Second World War. The visitor is cheered on his way by men and women who today help to make Scotch whisky for a thirsty world. On the way out there is a shop stocked with a variety of whiskies, both blends and single 'malts', books and other mementos.

The Centre is open seven days a week and is only closed on Christmas Day.

A member of the Town Guard in Edinburgh at the Scotch Whisky Heritage Centre, attempting in vain to prevent illicit whisky being smuggled into the city.

(Scotch Whisky Heritage Centre)

1. Rhyme to Henley in Janet Adam Smith, *Robert Louis Stevenson, Collected Poems*, Rupert Hart Davis, 1950, London.
2. George Saintsbury, *Works of Tobias Smollett*, Vol. 12, 1928, London.
3. Samuel Johnson, *A Journey to the Western Islands of Scotland*, 1985, Oxford.
4. Elizabeth Grant of Rothiemurchus, *Memoirs of a Highland Lady 1798–1827*, 1898, London.

SCOTCH WHISKY DISTILLERIES WHICH WELCOME VISITORS

DISTILLERY	HISTORY	TO VISIT	PROPRIETOR	TYPE
Scotch Whisky Heritage Centre 383 Castlehill Royal Mile Edinburgh		All year round, 7 days a week Tel: 031-220-0441		
Aberfeldy Distillery Aberfeldy Perthshire	Built 1896–8 by John Dewar & Sons	By prior appointment Tel: Aberfeldy 20330 Scottish Malt Distillers Ltd	John Dewar & Sons Ltd	Highland
Aberlour-Glenlivet Distillery Aberlour Banffshire	Founded 1826 by James Gordon	By appointment Tel: Aberlour 204	Aberlour-Glenlivet Distillery Co. Ltd	Highland
Auchroisk Distillery Mulben nr Keith Banffshire	Completed 1974 by International Distillers and Vintners	By appointment Tel: Mulben 333	Justerini & Brooks (Scotland) Ltd	Highland
Balmenach Distillery Cromdale Moray	Thought to have been founded by James MacGregor in 1824	By prior appointment Tel: Grantown on Spey 2569 Scottish Malt Distillers Ltd	John Crabbie & Co. Ltd	Highland
Blair Athol Distillery Pitlochry	In operation in 1798, revived in 1825–6 by John Robertson	By appointment. Visiting at 9.30am Fri–Mon (closed July and first week in August) Tel: 0796 2161	Arthur Bell & Sons plc	Highland
Bruichladdich Distillery Port Charlotte Isle of Islay	Built in 1881 by Robert, William and John Gourlay Harvey	By prior appointment Tel: Port Charlotte 221 Mr I. Allen	The Invergordon Distillers Ltd	Islay
Bunnahabhain Distillery Isle of Islay Argyllshire	Opened 1882 by the Islay Distillery Co.	Visitors welcome by prior appointment only Tel: 049 684 646	The Highland Distilleries Co. plc	Islay
Caol Ila Distillery Port Askaig Isle of Islay	Built 1846 by Hector Henderson	By prior appointment Tel: Port Askaig 207 Scottish Malt Distillers Ltd	Bulloch Lade & Co. Ltd	Islay
Cardhu Distillery Knockando Banffshire	Established 1824 by John Cumming	By prior appointment Tel: Carron 204 Scottish Malt Distillers Ltd	John Walker & Sons Ltd	Highland
Clynelish Distillery Brora Sutherland	Built 1967–8 by Scottish Malt Distilleries	By prior appointment Tel: Brora 21444 Scottish Malt Distillers Ltd	Ainslie & Heilbron (Distillers) Ltd	Highland
Cragganmore Distillery Ballindalloch Banffshire	Built 1869–70 by John Smith of Glenfarclas	By prior appointment Tel: Ballindalloch 202 Scottish Malt Distillers Ltd	D. & J. McCallum Ltd	Highland
Craigellachie Distillery Craigellachie Banffshire	Built 1891 by Craigellachie Distillery Co.	By prior appointment Tel: Craigellachie 212 Scottish Malt Distillers Ltd	White Horse Distillers Ltd	Highland
Dailuaine Distillery Carron Banffshire	Thought to have been built in 1852	By prior appointment Tel: Carron 361 Scottish Malt Distillers Ltd	Scottish Malt Distillers Ltd	Highland
Dallas Dhu Distillery Forres Moray	Built 1899 by Alexander Edward	No special appointment Open to visitors 1st April to 30th September, 10am to 7pm Tel: 0309 72802	Historic Buildings and Monuments Directorate of Scotland	Highland
Dalmore Distillery Alness Ross-shire	Founded 1839 by Alexander Matheson	Visitors accepted from 1st week in September until mid-June by prior arrangement on Monday, Tuesday or Thursday only at 11am or 2pm Tel: Alness 882 362 Distillery Manager, Mr J. P. Macdonald	Whyte & Mackay Distillers Ltd	Highland

Dalwhinnie Distillery Dalwhinnie Inverness-shire	Built 1897–8 by the Strathspey Distillery Co.	By prior appointment Tel: Dalwhinnie 264 Scottish Malt Distillers Ltd	James Buchanan & Co. Ltd	Highland
Fettercairn Distillery Fettercairn Kincardineshire	Founded 1824 by James Stewart	Visitors accepted from 1st week in September until mid- June by prior arrangement on Wednesdays only at 10.30am or 2pm Tel: Fettercairn 244 Distillery Manager, Mr Douglas Cooper	Whyte & Mackay Distillers Ltd	Highland
Glendronach Distillery Huntly Aberdeenshire	Founded 1826 by the Glendronach Distillery Co.	By appointment Tel: Forgue 202	The Glendronach Distillery Co. Ltd	Highland
Glendullan Distillery Dufftown Banffshire	Built 1897–8 by William Williams & Sons	By prior appointment Tel: Dufftown 20250 Scottish Malt Distillers Ltd	MacDonald Greenlees Ltd	Highland
Glen Elgin Distillery Longmorn Morayshire	Built 1898–1900 by William Simpson and James Carle	By prior appointment Tel: Longmorn 212 Scottish Malt Distillers Ltd	White Horse Distillers Ltd	Highland
Glenfarclas-Glenlivet Distillery Marypark Ballindalloch Banffshire	Founded 1836 by Robert Hay	No special appointment Open to visitors from 9.00– 4.30 Mon–Fri. Large parties please telephone in advance Tel: Ballindalloch 245	J. & G. Grant	Highland
Glenfiddich Distillery Dufftown Banffshire	Founded 1886–7 by William Grant & Sons	No special appointment Large parties please phone in advance Tel: Dufftown 20373	William Grant & Sons Ltd	Highland
Glengoyne Distillery Dumgoyne nr Killearn Stirlingshire	Founded in 1833	Guided tours at certain times Mon–Fri only. Large parties please phone in advance Tel: 041-332 6361	Lang Brothers Ltd	Highland
Glen Grant-Glenlivet Distillery Rothes Morayshire	Established 1840 by John Grant	Tel: Rothes 413 Visiting hours: Mon–Fri 10.00–4.00	J. & J. Grant (Glen Grant) Ltd	Highland
Glenkinchie Distillery Pencaitland East Lothian	In operation in 1837	By prior appointment Tel: Pencaitland 340 333 Scottish Malt Distillers Ltd	John Haig & Co. Ltd	Lowland
The Glenlivet Distillery Glenlivet Banffshire	Built 1858 by G. and J. G. Smith to replace their distilleries at Drummin and Delnabo	Tel: Glenlivet 427 Visiting hours 10.00–5.00 Mon–Sat	Geo. J. G. Smith Ltd.	Highland
Glenmorangie Distillery Tain Ross-shire	Converted 1843 from the Morangie brewery by William Mathieson	By prior appointment Tel: Tain 2043	Macdonald & Muir Ltd	Highland
Glenrothes Distillery Rothes Morayshire	Built 1878 by William Grant & Co.	By prior appointment with The Highland Distilleries Co. plc Glasgow Office: 041-332 7511	The Highland Distilleries Co. plc	Highland
Highland Park Distillery Kirkwall Orkney	Founded 1826 by Robert Borwick	Easter–end September 10.00– 16.00 hours, Mon–Fri only Other visits by prior arrangement Groups over 10 please phone in advance Tel: Kirkwall 4619	James Grant & Co. (Highland Park Distillery) Ltd	Islay
Isle of Jura Distillery Jura	Thought to have been founded 1810, in operation 1831–2	By appointment Tel: 049 682 240 Mr Tate	The Invergordon Distillers Ltd	Islay
Lagavulin Distillery Port Ellen Isle of Islay	Established in 1816 by John Johnston	By prior appointment Tel: Port Ellen 2400 Scottish Malt Distillers Ltd	White Horse Distillers Ltd	Islay

Laphroaig Distillery Port Ellen Isle of Islay	Supposed to have been founded in 1820, in operation by Donald Johnston in 1826	By appointment Tel: Port Ellen 2418 Visiting Tues and Thurs only 11.00 and 3.00	Long John Distilleries Ltd	Islay
Lochnagar Distillery Crathie Aberdeen-shire	Founded 1826 by James Robertson	By prior appointment Tel: Crathie 273 Scottish Malt Distillers Ltd	John Begg Ltd	Highland
Macallan-Glenlivet Distillery Craigellachie Morayshire	Founded 1824–5 by Alexander Reid	By appointment only Tel: Aberlour 471	Macallan-Glenlivet plc	Highland
Macduff Distillery Banff Banffshire	Built 1962–3 by Block, Grey & Block	By prior appointment Tel: Banff 2612	William Lawson Distillers Ltd	Highland
Miltonduff-Glenlivet Distillery Elgin Morayshire	Founded 1824–5 by Preavey & Bain	By appointment Tel: Elgin 7433	Hiram Walker & Sons (Scotland) plc	Highland
Oban Distillery Oban Argyllshire	Founded 1794 by Hugh, John, and James Stevenson	By prior appointment Tel: Oban 62110 Scottish Malt Distillers Ltd	John Hopkins & Co. Ltd	Highland
Ord Distillery Muir of Ord Ross-shire	Founded 1838 by the Ord Distillery Co.	By prior appointment Tel: Muir of Ord 870 421 Scottish Malt Distillers Ltd	John Dewar & Sons Ltd	Highland
Rosebank Distillery Falkirk Stirlingshire	Founded 1817–19 by James Robertson, moved to present site in 1840	By prior appointment Tel: Falkirk 23325 Scottish Malt Distillers Ltd	The Distillers Agency Ltd	Highland
Strathisla Distillery Keith Banffshire	Founded 1786 as Milltown distillery by George Taylor and Alexander Milne	By appointment. Open from mid-June to early September	Chivas Brothers Ltd	Highland
Talisker Distillery Carbost Isle of Skye	Founded 1831–2 by Hugh and Kenneth MacAskill	By prior appointment Tel: Carbost 203	John Walker & Sons Ltd	Islay
Tamdhu Distillery Knockando Morayshire	Built 1896–7 by the Tamdhu Distillery Co.	Easter–end September Mon–Sat Open from 10.00–16.00 hours. Simply turn up. Groups over 10 by appointment Tel: 034 06 221	The Highland Distilleries Co. plc	Highland
Tamnavulin-Glenlivet Distillery Tamnavulin Morayshire	Built 1965–6 by the Tamnavulin-Glenlivet Distillery Co.	By appointment Tel: Glenlivet 442 Mon–Fri afternoons only	The Invergordon Distillers Ltd	Highland
Tomatin Distillery Tomatin Inverness-shire	Founded 1897 by the Tomatin Spey District Distillery Co.	By appointment only Tel: Tomatin 234 – Mr John McDonald	Tomatin Distillers Co. Ltd	Highland
Tomintoul-Glenlivet Distillery Ballindalloch Banffshire	Built 1964–5 by the Tomintoul Distillery Ltd	Open from 1st week in September until mid-June by arrangement on Mon, Tues and Thurs only Tel: Glenlivet 274 – Distillery Manager, Mr Sandy Robertson	Whyte & Mackay Distillers Ltd	Highland
Tullibardine Distillery Blackford Perthshire	Reconstructed 1949	By appointment Mon–Fri afternoons only Tel: 076 482 252 – Mr B Kenny	The Invergordon Distillers Ltd	Highland

Select Bibliography

Andrews, Allen, *The Whisky Barons*, Jupiter Books, London, 1977

Barnard, Alfred, *The Whisky Distilleries of the United Kingdom*, 1887 (reprinted by Lochar Publishing in conjunction with Mainstream Publishing, Edinburgh, 1987)

Barnard, Alfred, *The Noted Breweries of Great Britain and Ireland*, London, 1891

Bell, Colin, *Famous Drambusters Guide – Scotch Whisky*, Lang Syne Publishers Ltd, Glasgow, 1985

Bremner, David, *The Industries of Scotland*, Edinburgh, 1869 (reprint David & Charles, Newton Abbot, 1973)

Brewer's Almanack, The Review Press Ltd, London

Brewer's Guardian, London

Brewery Manual, The Country Brewers' Gazette, London

Collison, Francis, *The Life and Times of William Grant*, William Grant & Sons Ltd, 1979

Cooper, Derek, *The Century Companion to Whiskies*, Century Publishing, London, 1978 and 1983

Daiches, David, *Scotch Whisky*, André Deutsch, London 1969 (republished with Fontana, London, 1983)

Donachie, Ian, *A History of the Brewing Industry in Scotland*, Edinburgh, 1979

Gunn, Neil, *Whisky and Scotland*, Routledge, London, 1935

Hume, John R., *Dallas Dhu Distillery*, HMSO, Edinburgh, 1988

Jackson, Michael, *The World Guide to Whisky*, Dorling Kindersley, London, 1987

Kay, Billy and MacLean, Cailean, *Knee Deep in Claret*, Mainstream Publishing, Edinburgh, 1983

Keir, David, *The Younger Centuries*, Edinburgh, 1981

Kenna, Rudolph and Mooncy, Anthony, *People's Palaces, the Victorian and Edwardian Pubs of Scotland*, Edinburgh, 1983

Lockhart, Sir R. Bruce, *Scotch – The Whisky of Scotland in Fact and Story*, Putnam, London 1959 & 1967

McDowall, R.J.S., revised by William Waugh, *The Whiskies of Scotland*, John Murray, London, 1986

McMaster, Charles, *Alloa Ale: a History of the Brewing Industry in Alloa*, Alloa, 1985

McNeill, F. Marian, *The Scots Cellar*, Edinburgh, 1956

Morrice, Philip, *The Schweppes Guide to Scotch*, Alpha Books, Sherbourne, 1983

Moss, Michael S., *The Story of Scotch Whisky – A Souvenir Guidebook to the Scotch Whisky Heritage Centre*, 1988

Moss, Michael S. and Hume, John R., *The Making of Scotch Whisky*, James & James, Edinburgh, 1981

Pigot's *Commercial Directory of Scotland*, Edinburgh, 1826–37

Sillet, Steve W., *Illicit Scotch*, Beaver Books, Aberdeen, 1965

Simpson, Bill, with others, *Scotch Whisky*, Macmillan, London, 1974

Spiller, Brian, *The Chameleon's Eye*, James Buchanan & Co, London and Glasgow, 1984

Weir, Ron B., *The History of the Pot Still Malt Distillers' Association of Scotland: The North of Scotland Malt Distillers Association, 1874–1926*, Elgin, 1970

Wilson, John, *Scotland's Malt Whiskies*, Famendam Publishers, Gartochan, 1974

Wilson, Neil, *Scotch and Water*, Lochar Publishing, Lockerbie, 1985

Wilson, Ross, *Scotch Made Easy*, Hutchison, London, 1959

Wilson, Ross, *Scotch – The Formative Years*, Constable, London, 1970

Wilson, Ross, *Scotch – its History and Romance*, David & Charles, Newton Abbot, 1973

Young, Jimmy, *A Short History of Ale*, David & Charles, Newton Abbot, 1979

Index

126